CULT FICTIONS

Cult Fictions follows the trail that led Jung to found the Psychological Club in Zurich in 1916. Leading Jung scholar Sonu Shamdasani recounts the controversies that ensued, and how Jung's followers reformulated his project. He assesses the evidence for the allegation that the Psychological Club was, in all but name, a cult founded upon the self-deification of Jung. Crucial new documents by Jung are published here for the first time. The detection work undertaken by the author shows that allegation to be erroneous and the result of mistaken identities.

Cult Fictions sets the record straight on Jung's aims and ambitions for psychology. Essential reading for anyone following contemporary debates on the legitimacy of analytical psychology and new religious movements, it addresses concerns over the institutionalisation of psychotherapy in general.

Sonu Shamdasani is an historian of psychology, and currently a research fellow at the Wellcome Institute for the History of Medicine, London. He is the editor of several books, including Jung's seminar, *The Psychology of Kundalini Yoga*, (Bollingen Series, Princeton University Press/Routledge).

CULT FICTIONS

C. G. Jung and the founding of analytical psychology

Sonu Shamdasani

London and New York

First published 1998 by Routledge
New Fetter Lane, London EC4P 4EE

Simultaneously published in the USA and Canada
by Routledge
29 West 35th Street, New York, NY 10001

©1998 Sonu Shamdasani

Typeset in Times by Routledge
Printed and bound in Great Britain by Clays Ltd, St. Ives PLC

British Library Cataloguing in Publication Data
A catalogue record for this book is available from the British Library

Library of Congress Cataloguing in Publication Data
Shamdasani, Sonu.
Cult fictions: C.G. Jung and the founding of analytical
psychology/Sonu Shamdasani.
Includes bibliographical references and index.
1. Psychoanalysis. 2. Jungian psychology. 3. Jung, C.G (Carl Gustav),
1875–1961. I. Title.
BF173.S486   1998   97–32830
150.19'5–dc21   CIP

ISBN–0 415 18613 7 (hbk)
ISBN–0 415 18614 5 (pbk)

For Maggie

CONTENTS

ACKNOWLEDGEMENTS

This work would not have been possible without assistance and support from many directions.

I would like to thank the following institutions and individuals for permission to reproduce published and unpublished work:

Niedieck Linder AG and the Erbengemeinschaft C. G. Jung for permission to cite excerpts from Jung's letters to Poul Bjerre, Michael Fordham, Ernest Jones and Alphonse Maeder, and to reproduce Jung's letter to the Executive committee of the Psychological Club, and his letter to the analysts of the Association for Analytical Psychology, and the unpublished section of his paper 'Individuation and collectivity' which appear here for the first time.

Excerpts from interviews in the Jung oral history archive, excerpts from Fanny Bowditch Katz's correspondence and diaries, are used with the permission of the Francis A. Countway Library of Medicine, and 'analytical collectivity' is reproduced with their permission.

I would like to thank Princeton University Press for permission to cite from Richard Noll's *The Jung Cult* and from Stuart Atkins' translation of *Faust*.

The heirs of Erna Wolff for permission to reproduce the photo of Jung by Erna Wolff which appears on the cover.

Paul Bishop and John Peck for permission to cite their letters to *The London Review of Books* and *Du* respectively.

I would like to thank the Wellcome Trust for funding the research on which this has been based. At the Wellcome Institute for the History of Medicine, Bill Bynum and Roy Porter have provided invaluable support and encouragement of my researches.

Whilst I have principally presented and discussed documentary evidence in this book, I am indebted to conversations and interviews which I have had over the last decade with individuals who knew

Jung, which have greatly informed me. In particular, I am grateful to the late Michael Fordham for discussing 'analytical collectivity' with me, and for his recollections of Jung and his views on the institutional development of analytical psychology from the 1930s to 1995.

Over the years, friends in Freud scholarship have provided a sustaining matrix for my work, through the integrity and exemplary quality of their research: Mikkel Borch-Jacobsen, Ernst Falzeder, Richard Skues, Anthony Stadlen and Peter Swales.

I would like to thank Angela Graf-Nold and Anatina Weiser for discussions concerning the early history of psychoanalysis, analytical psychology and psychiatry in Switzerland, and the latter for providing me with obituaries of Franz Riklin.

At critical moments in this project, Jay Livernois and Andrew Samuels provided advice and encouragement which enabled it to move forward. Amy Lenzo's assistance with the transcription of Fanny Bowditch Katz's diaries was of great assistance.

The comments on the manuscript of Natalie Baron, Mikkel Borch-Jacobsen, Ernst Falzeder, Jay Sherry and Richard Skues have greatly enriched it.

Research in Switzerland was facilitated by invitations by Vincent Barras and Fernando Vidal to address their seminar in the history and philosophy of science at the University of Geneva in 1995 and 1996, and an invitation by Vincent Barras and Jacques Gasser to speak at the conference, 'Histoire de la psychiatrie: nouvelles approches, nouvelles perspectives,' at the Institut Romand d'Histoire de la Médecine et de la Santé in Lausanne and Geneva in 1997. I would also like to thank Andreas and Angela Graf-Nold for their hospitality in Zurich.

Research in the USA was facilitated by the invitation of John Beebe, Joseph Cambray and Coline Covington to speak at the *Journal of Analytical Psychology*'s 1997 conference in Maine, 'Family Matters: The Descendants of Freud and Jung.' I would also like to thank Eugene Taylor for his hospitality in Boston, and a continuing conversation concerning Jung and the history of psychology stretching back many years.

At Routledge, I would like to thank Edwina Welham for grasping the significance of this project, and enabling its swift publication.

Responsibility for the views expressed in this book are my own.

1

CULT AND ASSOCIATION

> I was nobody: I might have turned out to be a country
> doctor. A man finds himself singled out, isolated and alone:
> People are attracted and come.
>
> (Jung to Edward Thornton, 1951)[1]

What is a psychological association? From the inception of modern
psychotherapy, this question has never ceased to be asked, whatever
the particular therapeutic school. Should psychotherapists organise
themselves according to a traditional model? Or was there something
within the very nature of the psychotherapeutic enterprise and its
understanding of human relations that contained the conception of a
new form of social order? If so, how was this to be implemented?
These questions were not simply limited to the issue of how
psychotherapists should arrange their institutions, but had bearings
on whether they could make wider contributions to society. Modern
psychotherapy held out the promise of a deeper understanding of
human nature than had previously been possible. It was hoped that
this would in turn lead to a new era of transformed social relations.
There has been no end of psychologies of the nursery, of school, of
industry, of corporate life, of the nation and international relations
propounded this century. There has been no form of social organisation that has not – for better or worse – met with an attempted
psychological reformulation. Today, the institutions of psychotherapy
are undergoing a legitimation crisis, and the societal legacies of
psychotherapy are increasingly contested. Hence it is important to
consider their historical genesis.

At the beginning of the twentieth century psychotherapy assumed
the traditional medical model of one-to-one private practice. It

---

1 Cited in Edward Thornton, *The Diary of a Mystic*, p. 134.

established its own institutions, distinct from the medical schools and the university, which became the operative bases of modern psychology and psychiatry. A principal figure in these institutional developments was C. G. Jung. During his association with Freud, he was a prime architect of the International Psychoanalytic Movement. Psychoanalysis truly became international with the arrival of the Zurich school. It was Jung, the first president of the International Psychoanalytical Association, who organised its first congresses and established its first journal. As Freud recalled:

> Nowhere else did such a compact little group of adherents exist, or could a public clinic be placed at the service of psychoanalytic researches, or was there a clinical teacher who included psychoanalytic theories as an integral part of his psychiatric course. The Zurich group thus became the nucleus of the small band who were fighting for the recognition of analysis. The only opportunity of learning the new art and working at it in practice lay there. Most of my followers and co-workers at the present time came to me by way of Zurich, even those who were geographically much nearer to Vienna than Switzerland.[2]

For psychiatrists interested in psychoanalysis, it was Zurich and not Vienna that was initially the instruction centre of choice. As Ernst Falzeder points out, many significant figures in dynamic psychiatry and psychoanalysis either worked at or visited the Burghölzli:

> Karl Abraham, Roberto Greco Assagioli, Ludwig Binswanger, Abraham Arden Brill, Trigant Burrow, Imre Décsi, Max Eitingon, Sándor Ferenczi, Otto Gross, August Hoch, Johann Jakob Honegger, Smith Ely Jelliffe, Ernest Jones, Alphonse Maeder, Hans Meier, Hermann Nunberg, Johan H. W. van Ophuijsen, Nikolai J. Ossipow, Frederick Peterson, Franz Riklin, Hermann Rorschach, Tatiana Rosenthal, Leonhard Seif, Eugénie Soloknicka, Sabina Spielrein, Fülöp Stein, Wolf Stockmayer, Johannes Irgens

---

2 Freud, 'On the history of the psycho-analytic movement', *SE* 14, p. 27. The implications of this statement for the historiography of psychoanalysis have yet to be fully grasped.

Stromme, Jaroslaw Stuchlick and G. Alexander Young – and this list is certainly by no means complete.[3]

This gives some indication of the critical role played by the Burghölzli in instigating the development of a psychogenic orientation in psychiatry.

It was Jung who first introduced the rite of training analysis, stipulating that any would-be analyst would first have to submit to analysis. This has become the one standard feature in the plethora of psychotherapeutic schools in the twentieth century. Like psychoanalysis, analytical psychology came to organise itself around training institutes. By contrast, alongside these institutes there were also organisations comprising a combination of lay and professional members called Clubs. These continue to exist to this day.[4] While the conditions of membership for these clubs vary, they generally include the requirement of members having had some Jungian analysis. Given the historical and social transformations that analytical psychology has undergone, it would be a mistake to conflate in any way the present Clubs with their predecessors. The peripheralisation of the Clubs has been a major factor in the development of the modern profession of analytical psychology.

A distinctive feature of Jung's work was its attempt to provide psychological understanding of the processes of personality transformation which he claimed underlay religious, hermetic, gnostic and alchemical practices. He developed these at a time when such subjects were dismissed out of hand by the positivist and behaviourist approach dominant in psychology, or were reduced by psychoanalysis to nothing but psychopathology. For many, his non-derisive attention to such subjects was enough to brand him as an occultist, a charge which he persistently denied. In the fifties, Henri Ellenberger noted apropos Jung's detractors: 'The adversaries of Jung accuse him

---

3 Ernst Falzeder, 'The threads of psychoanalytic filiations or psychoanalysis taking effect', p. 172. This landmark paper marks the beginning of the social history of the development of the psychoanalytic movement.

4 For an overview of some of these developments, see Andrew Samuels, ' "A Jung Club is not enough": The professionalisation of Analytical Psychology 1913–1957 and its implications for today'. A history of analytical psychology, which is much needed, is currently being undertaken by Thomas Kirsch. On the organisation of psychoanalysis, see Gerhard Wittenberger, *Das 'Geheime Komitee' Sigmund Freuds: Institionalisierungsprozesse in der Psychoanalytischen Bewegung zwischen 1912 und 1927*, and my 'Psychoanalysis Inc'.

of having revived old gnostic or theosophical systems under a psychological disguise'.[5] Nor were such statements only made from a negative perspective; many proponents of the Perennial Philosophy, Hermeticism, Gnosticism, Alchemy and Magic were quick to claim Jung as one of their own and use his name to lend credibility and legitimacy to their ideas. Hence the widespread presence of works on Jungian psychology in occult bookshops, amidst the amulets, incense, crystals and New Age music. The one academic field in which Jung's work has been most engaged with is that of religious studies. It has been claimed that 'no psychologist of religion has influenced contemporary scholars of comparative religion more than Carl Gustav Jung'.[6]

After Jung, possibly the first to draw a parallel between the practices of analytical psychology and ancient mystery cults was the analytical psychologist C. A. Meier, in his *Ancient Incubation and Modern Psychotherapy* (1949). He claimed that Jung had made psychological discoveries which offered close contact with the ancient healing cults.[7] These were, that the psyche has a religious function, and that in the second half of life healing consisted in experiencing this. Meier raised the question of whether modern psychotherapy was a cult. Jungian psychology, he recounted, had often been accused of being a cult and an esoteric secret society.[8] He argued that this was not the case, because Jung had 'labored unremittingly to describe and elaborate the result of his research and practice'.[9] For Meier, the extent to which Jung had striven to make public his findings indicated that analytical psychology was not an esoteric secret society.

Controversy has raged concerning the nature and legitimacy of the institutions of psychoanalysis and analytical psychology from their inception. In 1953 Henri Ellenberger characterised the newly founded Jung Institute in Zurich in the following way:

I do not know any place where one breathes the atmosphere

---

5 Ellenberger, 'La psychiatrie suisse, (III)' p. 151. Unless otherwise indicated, all translations are my own.
6 Martin Wulff, *Psychology of Religion: Classic and Contemporary Views*, p. 411. Wulff gives a useful overview of the reception of Jung's psychology of religion.
7 C. A. Meier, *Ancient Incubation and Modern Psychotherapy*, p. 123.
8 *Ibid.*
9 *Ibid.*

of a 'theosophical sect' more stiflingly than at the Jung
Institute in Zurich – no other chapel where the master is
more divinised or is becoming so. Many of the disciples of
Jung openly devote themselves to astrology, to occultism and
to divination with the aid of the Chinese oracle, the I Ching.
It is often maintained that Jung has, apart from his official
doctrine, an esoteric doctrine, following the example of the
ancient philosophies, which he always denies.[10]

The characterisation of analytical psychology as occult or esoteric
went hand in hand with the designation of the Jung institute as a sect
or a cult.

During the same period, Michael Fordham, the leading analytical
psychologist in Britain, noted the existence of a cultic tendency in
analytical psychology, which he strove to oppose. Fordham was in
personal contact with Jung from 1935 until Jung's death.[11] He saw
this tendency as *diametrically opposed to Jung's own intentions*:

> I became very aware of the tendency of analytical psychology
> to become a quasi-religious cult, not at all Jung's idea as I
> understood him both from his writings and personally.[12]

10 Ellenberger, 'La psychiatrie suisse (VI)' p. 306. At the same time, he differentiated
between Jung, whom he held in great esteem, and some of his followers: 'Most of
those who have had personal contact with Jung, however brief, agree on the fascinating side of his personality (often compared to that of a magician): in his
conversation, the most profound, the most subtle and sometimes the most para-
doxical views follow one another with an incomparable ease and rapidity. One
finds a reflection of this in his works, above all in the published lectures, in the
measure to which the text does not move away too much from the original spontaneity. On the other hand, he who has had the privilege of a personal
conversation with Jung can only be distressed at the sight of the sad and ultra-
schematic "resumés" of his doctrine published by certain of his pupils . . . '. 'La
psychiatrie suisse (III)' *Evolution Psychiatrique* 1952, p. 154.
11 On Fordham's work, see James Astor, *Michael Fordham: Innovations in Analytical
Psychology*, and my introduction to his *Analyst–Patient Interaction: Collected
Papers on Technique*.
12 Michael Fordham, *Explorations into the Self*, p. 2. In 1942 Fordham wrote in a
letter to the *British Medical Journal* replying to a review of Jolande Jacobi's *The
Psychology of C. G. Jung*: 'there is no reason to think that Jung's work has
produced something that is even "in some ways . . . more a religion than a science".
Jung is simply a student of human nature, and his work is neither more nor less
scientific than that of others who are interested in the same subject. . . . He has no

It was explicitly to combat this tendency that Fordham wrote a series of essays which became the volume *The Objective Psyche* (1958). In his memoirs, Fordham expanded on this theme:

> My personal relation with him [Jung] made me aware of a trend amongst some of his followers, and his detractors as well, which he deplored. It hinted that analytical psychology was a sort of religion.[13]

For Fordham, some of Jung's followers were responsible for attempting to turn analytical psychology into a quasi-religious cult, but not Jung himself.[14] This distinction is critical.[15]

In a little-known book in 1976, James Webb attempted to locate Jung's work in the context of the turn of the century occult revival. Webb claimed that for many, Jung's psychology restated ideas at the centre of the occult tradition in a manner accessible to those who were uneasy with religious language.[16] He argued that there were many affinities between Jung's work and that of the religious elements of the occult revival:

> It is certain that the tradition to which Jung belonged was obvious to fellow-adepts, who came to Jung as the preferred modern interpreter of traditional metaphysics. From such

more created a religion than have the anthropologists'. (29 August 1942, p. 260). In his introduction to *The Objective Psyche*, he wrote that it was individuals who were 'overawed by the numinous character of archetypal images' who believed in analytical psychology as a religion (p. 1).

13 Fordham, *The Making of an Analyst: A Memoir*, p. 117.

14 On one occasion, I read Fordham a letter from Jung to Ernest Jones of 7 May 1913 in which he wrote: 'I am not in love with my ideas. I just consider them as working hypotheses and not as eternal truths'. (Sigmund Freud Copyrights). He laughed and said that that was precisely what some of the Jungians had turned them into. In his memoirs he stated that when Culver Barker, Gerhard and Hella Adler, Erna Rosenbaum and Vera von der Heydt set up the Association for Jungian Analysts in London in opposition to the Society of Analytical Psychology, they were 'in serious danger of forming a Jungian creed which Jung himself would have abhorred'. *The Making of an Analyst*, p. 135. On the history of these acrimonious splits, see Ann Casement, 'A brief history of Jungian splits in the United Kingdom'.

15 I have elsewhere commented on the posthumous canonisation of Jung. See my 'Memories, Dreams, Omissions', p. 122.

16 James Webb, *The Occult Establishment*, p. 387.

contact with like-minded spirits, Jung must have derived stimulus, inspiration, and ideas.[17]

Webb's work was important in drawing attention to areas and connections that had not received much attention. Unfortunately, his reconstruction of Jung's relations with other figures was at times excessively speculative and inferential.

In the same year as Webb's study, Paul Stern published his *C. G. Jung: The Haunted Prophet*, in which he alleged that the founding of the Psychological Club in Zurich in 1916 amounted to the inauguration of a sect.[18] He claimed that the theories of analytical psychology represented the mythologisation of Jung's psychosis. Jung was a would-be prophet disguised behind the mantle of a scientist, around whom followers gathered in a hero cult. The Jung Institute in Zurich was Jung's 'mystical body'.

In the last half century the basic templates of how Jung's work has been received have changed very little. The charges of the revival of ancient philosophical and religious systems in a modern guise and the characterisation of the founding of the Psychological Club as marking the formation of the cult or sect of the Jungian movement have in turn been recently revived by Richard Noll in *The Jung Cult* and *The Aryan Christ*. In particular, some of Noll's statements are strikingly reminiscent of that of Webb. One new twist is Noll's claim to have provided previously unknown *prima facie* evidence that Jung himself had formed a cult in the form of a misidentified text at the Countway library in Boston.[19] He claims that this text was actually Jung's inaugural address at the founding of his cult – otherwise known as the Psychological Club in Zurich in 1916. The existence of a secret founding text would lend credence to the belief that there was an esoteric doctrine at the core of analytical psychology and its institutional organisation – as some have alleged previously. Were it not for this text and the claims made upon it, there is little in Noll's work that would merit further attention.[20] For these considerations

---

17 *Ibid.*, p. 393.
18 'The founding of the Jungian club meant the social embodiment of Jungian psychology, the genesis of a sect'. Paul Stern, *C. G. Jung: The Haunted Prophet*, p. 153.
19 For the full text, see Appendix one.
20 In recent years, several books on Jung have appeared which have made far more important historical contributions than Noll's: Paul Bishop's *The Dionysian Self: C.G. Jung's Reception of Nietzsche,* F.X. Charet's *Spiritualism and the Foundations*

fundamentally affect not only how one views the founding of analytical psychology but also how one understands Jung's conception of the psychological enterprise. Hence the documentary basis for such claims is worthy of detailed scrutiny to enable an accurate reconstruction of the history of analytical psychology and its societal legacy.

In the *New York Times* Noll likens Jung to David Koresch, Jim Jones and Luc Jouret, and describes analytical psychology as a 'Swiss cult of middle-class, sun-worshipping neopagans led by a charismatic man who experienced himself to be Christ'.[21] Assertive utterance, however unfounded, quickly finds echoes amongst both champions and critics.[22] The statement that analytical psychology represented a neopagan sun-worshipping cult went beyond the more commonly expressed notion that there is something 'cult-like' about it. There is all the difference in the world between analogy and identity.

'Cults' are in. As Michael Hersch put it in *Newsweek*, there is today a worldwide pandemic of cults. Some also speak of a worldwide 'anti-cult crusade'.[23] Given this, it is unsurprising that Noll's sensational claims, which resonate with a widespread academic condemnation of Jung, would garner attention and occasion controversy. The cover of section two of the *Independent* for 1 October 1996 bore a full page portrait of the elderly Jung with the caption 'Is this the face of one of the century's most sinister cult leaders?' The occasion was a review of the British paperback edition of *The Jung Cult*. However, it is one thing to suggest that analytical psychology, as Jung conceived it, contained important esoteric dimensions. It is another to identify correctly what these are.

The term cult is bandied about so often today as to lose all meaning. As early as 1926, H. W. Fowler stated apropos its usage:

of *C.G. Jung's Psychology*, Ann Lammers' *In God's Shadow: The Collaboration between Victor White and C. G. Jung*, Magnus Ljunggren's *The Russian Mephisto. A Study of the life of Emilii Medtner*, and Marilyn Nagy's *Philosophical Issues in the Psychology of C.G. Jung.* None of these works have received the attention they deserve.

21 Noll, 'The rose, the cross and the analyst'.
22 Thus Anthony Storr, while criticising Noll's claims, states 'Richard Noll . . . prints a recently discovered document which appears to be a transcript of Jung's address inaugurating the first Jungian association, the Psychological Club in Zurich'. *Feet of Clay: A Study of Gurus*, p. 95. As we shall see, the Psychological Club was by no means the first Jungian association.
23 Michael Hersch, 'Worldwide, it's the "rush hour of the Gods": a clamor for cultic meaning in a society gone secular', p. 19. Irving Hexham and Karla Poewe, *New Religions and Global Cultures*, p. 1.

cult, as now used, dates only from the middle of last century; its proper place is in books on archaeology, comparative religion, & the like; that it should be ousting *worship* in general use is regrettable; . . .[24]

Before its adoption by scholars of comparative religion and sociologists, the term 'cult' was widely used by Christian theologians in the nineteenth century to designate heterodox tendencies and non-Christian religions.[25] In current usage the term commonly carries the opprobrium of 'false', as opposed to 'genuine', religion, and the secular condemnation of the irrational (both connotations appear to be present in Noll's depictions of the 'Jung cult'). Many scholars consequently prefer to speak more neutrally of new or alternate religious movements. Thus in Mircea Eliade's massive *Encyclopaedia of Religion*, one simply finds the following one line entry on the subject of cults: '*See* Community; New Religions; *and* Religious Communities, *article on* Religion, Community, and Society'.[26]

What is clear is that the term cult has today become a confused sign of a widespread questioning of the legitimacy of religious institutions, as witnessed for instance by the controversies surrounding the status of Scientology. Is it a form of psychotherapy, as was debated in the United Kingdom in the House of Commons, and is it a legitimate religion, as is being asked at the current time in Germany?[27] Thus the question of what a psychological association is, converges with the question, what is a religion? This last question was also a critical one for Jung, and at the centre of his psychology of religion. An account of this is beyond the present brief, and will be taken up on a later occasion.

There are many different ways of understanding cults. Noll puts forward two definitions of the term. The first, from Wilhelm Bousset, describes a cult as 'a community gathered for worship'.[28] The second, which he takes from Marc Galanter, describes it as:

---

24 H. W. Fowler, *A Dictionary of Modern English Usage*, pp. 100–1.

25 On the history of the usages of the term, see Irving Hexham and Karla Poewe, *New Religions and Global Cultures*, pp. 27–37.

26 Mircea Eliade (ed), *The Encyclopaedia of Religion*, vol. 4, p. 172.

27 See John Foster, *Enquiry into the Practice and Effects of Scientology*.

28 Marc Galanter, *Cults: Faith, Healing and Coercion*, p. 9. Cited in Noll, *The Jung Cult*, p. 16.

a charismatic group consisting of a dozen or so members, even hundreds or thousands. It is characterised by the following psychological elements: members (1) have a *shared belief system*, (2) sustain a high level of *social cohesiveness*, (3) are strongly influenced by the group's *behavioral norms*, and (4) impute *charismatic (or sometimes divine) power* to the group or its leadership.[29]

One can accept these definitions simply for the purpose of argument and consider to what extent the formation of the Psychological Club in 1916 constituted the inauguration of a cult – the Jung cult. Noll goes way beyond stating that the Jung cult was based on Jung's charisma. In Noll's view, it was based on nothing less than Jung's self-deification as the Aryan Christ. If this were the case it would have tremendous ramifications for how one understands the development of analytical psychology and its place in twentieth century society. If one is claiming that thousands of individuals over the last three quarters of a century have been completely mistaken in who they have taken Jung to be, it would be customary to have an abundance of supporting evidence. It is important to cross-examine the evidence for such claims – that is, of course, if there actually turns out to be any.

A great deal of the controversy around Jung's work has been because he was one of the most prominent modern psychologists to affirm religious values. In an often cited phrase, he stated that all of the patients coming to him in the second half of life principally suffered from a loss of religious meaning.[30] Jung's work on psychology and religion not only occasioned the scorn of secular critics, it also evoked much controversy from within religious communities. Some saw Jung's work as representing the unwelcome encroachment of psychology onto sacred terrain. Others viewed him as attempting to turn psychology into a religion. On several occasions, Jung explicitly denied that he had founded a religion. In 1936, he gave a talk in which he directly took up the frequently posed question of whether analytical psychology was a religion. In conclusion, he claimed:

---

29 *Ibid*, pp. 16–17.
30 Jung, 'The relation of psychotherapy to the cure of souls', (1932) *CW* 11, § 509. At the risk of confusion, I have given a literal rendition of Jung's original title. This paper was titled 'Psychotherapists or the clergy' in the Collected Works.

I am speaking just as a philosopher. People call me a religious leader. I am not that. I have no message, no mission; I attempt only to understand. We are philosophers in the old sense of the word, lovers of wisdom. That avoids the sometimes questionable company of those who offer a religion.[31]

Replying to Martin Buber's critique of his work, Jung wrote:

With this I preach no new religion, since for that I would have to at least – according to traditional custom – appeal to a divine revelation. I am essentially a physician, who has to do with the sickness of man and his times.[32]

On the contrary, he claimed that the value of his psychology of religion was its capacity to revivify religious traditions. It was towards the revitalisation of Christianity in particular that Jung dedicated a large share of his later work.[33] Furthermore, Jung affirmed his Christian identity on numerous occasions. He described himself to the Reverend H. L. Philp as being 'definitely inside Christianity' and as a 'Protestant in my soul and my body'.[34] He also described himself as being 'on the extreme left wing in the parliament of Protestant opinion'.[35] According to Noll, both Christianity and psychology were simply masks that Jung hid behind to conceal his paganism.[36]

Although there is nothing new in claims about the cult status of Jung's psychology, statements such as these raise an old argument to

---

31 Jung, 'Is analytical psychology a religion?', in William McGuire and R. F. C. Hull (eds), *C. G. Jung Speaking: Interviews and Encounters*, p. 98.

32 Jung, 'A reply to Martin Buber', (1952) *CW* 18, § 1511, tr. mod. In a letter to Herr Irminger, Jung wrote: 'I have neither the capacity nor the desire to be a founder of a religion [Religionsstifter]'. *Letters 1*, 22 September 1944, p. 346, tr. mod. According to Noll, Jung had formed a new religion in 1912, *The Aryan Christ*, p. 185.

33 To the Reverend David Cox, Jung wrote: 'It is my practical experience that psychological understanding immediately revivifies the essential Christian ideas and fills them with the breath of life'. 25 September 1957, *CW* 18, § 1666.

34 Jung to Reverend H. L. Philp, 26 October, 1956, pp. 334–5, *Letters 2*. To Herr Irminger, Jung said of himself: 'As a Christian, of course, I take my stand on the Christian truth', 22 September, 1944, *Letters 1*, p. 346. Noll claims that by the end of 1912 Jung had stopped regarding himself as a Christian, *The Aryan Christ*, p. 171.

35 Jung, 'The relation of psychotherapy to the cure of souls', *CW* 11, § 537.

36 Noll, *The Aryan Christ*, pp. xv–xvi, 160, 171.

a new pitch: as such, they represent some of the most absurd notions ever held about him and betray a failure to comprehend his work.

To state that Jung formed a cult based on his own self-deification requires that one discounts Jung's own testimony on this matter as unreliable, inherently deceptive and the mark of bad faith. Indeed, Noll claims that Jung 'confused' and 'deliberately misled' his followers.[37] This issue is critical: it is hard to see how one can square Jung's own statements that he did not form a religion with Noll's allegations that he formed a cult based on his self-deification. If one believes, as Noll is reported to, that Jung was 'the most influential liar of the twentieth century', then naturally one would attribute little weight to any of his statements.[38] One wonders what criteria were used to arrive at this condemnation. However, it is preferable to proceed on the assumption that good grounds have to be given on a case-by-case basis to justify dismissing statements as falsehoods. Otherwise, one is simply free to say whatever one likes about Jung (which, all too often, is precisely what happens). The most curious aspect of the reception of Jung's work is that there have been few figures in twentieth century intellectual history who have been subject to such a high level of misunderstanding. The misinterpretations of Jung show no signs of abating. Few psychologists continue to be so frequently fictionalised. Jung is continually being reinvented and stereotypically remodelled. This not only occurs in the constant stream of novels and plays relating to him, but also in works purporting to be scholarly. The latter are more dangerous for the unsuspecting, as their fictions are harder to detect.

---

37 *Ibid.*, p. 172.
38 Cited in Dinitia Smith, 'Scholar who says Jung lied is at war with descendants', *New York Times*, p. 9.

2

A CASE OF MISTAKEN IDENTITY?

How did it all begin? Noll claims that the prototype of the Jung cult was established in 1912, with the foundation in Zurich of the Society for Psychoanalytic Endeavours. That same year, a heated public debate in the newspapers concerning psychoanalysis took place.[1] According to Noll, these controversies drew Jung's disciples together and enhanced their social cohesiveness.[2] No evidence is provided for this supposition. He cites Jung's letter to Freud in which he conveyed news of the founding of this association:

> Another piece of news worth mentioning is the founding of a lay association for ψa efforts. The association numbers around 20 members, and only analysed persons are admitted. The founding occurred due to the wish of former patients. The rapport among the members of the association was acclaimed. I myself have still not attended a meeting. The chairman is a member of the ψa association. The attempt seems to be interesting from the standpoint of the question of the social application of ψa[tic] education.[3]

---

1 For an account of these debates, see Ellenberger, *The Discovery of the Unconscious*, pp. 811–14.
2 Noll, *The Jung Cult*, p. 194.
3 Jung to Freud, 25 February 1912, *Freud/Jung Letters*, p. 487, tr. mod. (ψa was used as a shorthand for psychoanalysis). Noll drew attention to the fact that Jung purportedly referred to this association in the same way as he would later refer to the club – as an experiment, *The Jung Cult*, p. 194. The term Jung actually used in this letter was 'der Versuch'. Whilst this can mean experiment, it more usually means attempt. In his subsequent reference to the Psychological Club in his foreword to Toni Wolff's *Studies in C. G. Jung's Psychology*, Jung referred to the Club as 'ein Experiment'. It was Richard Hull, and not Jung, who used the same word on both occasions.

13

So Jung was not even present at the inaugural meeting for what is supposed to have been the prototype of his cult! As Jung reports to Freud, the impetus for the association did not come from himself or Franz Riklin, but from former patients. Thus this association appears to be one of the first patient networks in the history of modern psychotherapy. The Korrespondenzblatt of the IPA carried the following notice (which Noll does not quote) announcing the formation of the society and describing its aims:

> On the 13th February 1912 a particular society was founded from the inspiration of the circle of the analysed with presently around 20 members, which, in accordance with the Zurich psychoanalytic association, dedicates itself to the cultivation of psychoanalysis. It should fulfil a double mission: first, to give the analysed, who mostly keep a permanent interest in analysis, the opportunity for further training and activity, and to create a milieu which for many should form a substitute for the previous one that had to be left behind with the neurosis as inopportune. Secondly, a permanent place for the cultivation and dissemination of analytical knowledge should be made for suitable interested people. Membership is granted only to the analysed for all sorts of practical reasons. The chairman is a member of the Zurich psychoanalytical association, presently Dr. Riklin. Meetings will be held every 14 days, alternating with the psychoanalytical association.[4]

The aims of this organisation sound much like any other designed to bring together people who share common interests and experiences.

Riklin had been a colleague and a collaborator of Jung's since the time they worked together in the Burghölzli. Despite the fact that Franz Riklin was the chairman, Noll simply asserts that 'it was Jung who was the true leader of this group'.[5] He goes on to claim that this association supplied the first evidence of a charismatic group centred on Jung and the nucleus of the Jung cult.[6]

---

4 *Zentralblatt für Psychoanalyse* 2, 1912, p. 480.
5 Noll, *The Jung Cult*, p. 196. In *The Aryan Christ*, Noll asserts that the group was set up by Jung and Riklin (pp. 167–8). There is no evidence that Jung had anything to do with the establishment of this organisation.
6 *Ibid.*, p. 197.

Or does it? From the list of lectures presented before the Society for Psychoanalytic Endeavours printed in the Korrespondenzblatt, it appears that Jung gave one talk on the 24th January 1913, on 'The unconscious psychology of Negroes'.[7] There is no firm evidence that he even attended any other meeting of this society. Noll's claim that this society was centred around Jung is flatly contradicted by the first-hand testimony of Heinrich Steiger, a member of this group. Steiger was analysed by Riklin and served on the executive of the Club from 1919 to 1957, first as secretary, and then as treasurer. In his interview in the Jung oral history archive Steiger recalled:

> Then one year after the war broke out, I read in an analytical paper or in an analytical journal 'There exists a circle guided by Dr. Riklin who assembles former analyzed persons, etc.', and I asked him if I could also join this circle.[8]

According to Steiger, there were *two* groups: Jung's and Riklin's. The latter group was invited to join the Club:

> There were two circles. The one was the circle who had gathered around Jung and had great lectures and meetings in his house at Küsnacht. . . . These two groups together made the Club.[9]

In her oral history interview, Suzanne Trüb, another member of this group and the sister of Toni Wolff and wife of Hans Trüb recalled:

> We were a small circle. Without Jung (the members were) Dr. Riklin, my sister, and the somewhat important persons of that time; we came together. And there also my husband and I attended.[10]

Riklin was also a talented painter, and increasingly forsook

---

7 Details were given of fifteen meetings from November 1912 onward. Herbert Oczeret gave the most talks (three).
8 Heinrich Steiger interview, Jung oral history archive, Countway Library of Medicine, Harvard (hereafter CLM), p. 9. He presumably refers to the notice in the *Zentralblatt* cited above.
9 *Ibid.*
10 Suzanne Trüb interview 2b, CLM, p. 9.

psychiatry for painting. After the First World War, he had a small private practice and dedicated himself to art. Heinrich Steiger recalled:

> That gave a split in him. It was a very tragic thing that because of that he lost his balance; because the painting did not bring money. So he was split between painting and psychiatry . . . he was splitting up and this disassociation of him had not given pleasure to Jung . . . the financial situation of Riklin was a narrow one at the end of his life. Because he didn't seriously work as a medical doctor and more in painting, etc., so he lost the big office. This was a tragic thing.[11]

In a passage omitted from the English edition of *Memories, Dreams, Reflections*, Jung spoke of a colleague of his who had been persuaded by the 'anima voice' patient that he was an artist:

> In reality the female patient whose voice spoke in me exercised a disastrous influence on men. She succeeded in talking a colleague of mine into believing that he was a misunderstood artist. He believed it and was shattered. The cause of his breakdown? He did not live from his own recognition but from the recognition of others. That is dangerous. This made him insecure and open to the insinuations of the anima; since what she says is often of a seductive power and a hidden cunning.[12]

Riklin's dual career as a psychiatrist and a painter, together with the correspondence between Jung's recollections and Steiger's, indicate that Riklin was the colleague in question. I have elsewhere suggested that the case for Maria Moltzer (of whom more later) being the woman in question is significantly stronger than that for Sabina Spielrein, as has been commonly argued.[13]

---

11 Steiger interview, CLM, pp. 8–11.
12 Jung, *Erinnerungen, Träume, Gedanken*, p. 190. On the history of the composition of this text, and how it became falsely perceived to be Jung's autobiography, see my 'Memories, dreams, omissions', and Alan Elms' 'The auntification of Jung' in *Uncovering Lives: The Uneasy Alliance of Biography and Psychology*.
13 See my 'Memories, dreams, omissions', p. 129. On the case for Spielrein as being this woman, see John Kerr, *A Most Dangerous Method*, pp. 502–7

Paul Stern also stated that Riklin had a circle of pupils and ex-patients which met at the Café 'Karl der Grosse', which Jung occasionally attended.[14] According to Steiger the initial membership of the Club was made up through the joining together of Jung's and Riklin's groups. This point is rather important, as one would assume that the identity of the figure at the centre of a cult is not an inessential aspect of it. It is hard to see how this could have been the prototype of the Jung cult if it was actually centred around Riklin (unless the latter was some kind of John the Baptist paving the way for the greater glory of Jung – which would have to be shown).[15] Consequently, Steiger's account does not bear out Noll's claim that the Society for Psychoanalytic Endeavours was the Ur-Jung Cult. Of course, Steiger could have been lying to disguise the true nature of the association, or simply misremembering. However, without other accounts of the society, one must surely give more credence to Steiger's testimony than to Noll's speculations. As we shall see, this is not the only instance of mistaken identity that Noll makes.

So far, Noll's reconstruction of the genesis of the Jung cult is not faring too well. At this stage he introduces the pivotal inaugural text. Before considering this text it is important to sketch out the actual origins of the Club.

---

14 Stern, *C. G. Jung: The Haunted Prophet*, p. 144. Stern provides an anecdote of one occasion on which Jung attended a meeting of Riklin's group.
15 For a critique of another conflation of Jung with Riklin, see my 'De Genève à Zürich: Jung et la Suisse Romande', p. 919. Concerning Riklin, Noll has the following footnote: 'On Riklin, see Dieter Baumann, "In Memory of Franz Riklin", *Spring* (1970)' *The Jung Cult*, p. 351. If one reads this piece, one sees that it is an obituary of Franz Riklin Jr., the son of the Riklin in question. One would have thought that an obituary of the man himself would have been more apposite. See the *Berner Tagblatt*, 13 December 1938 and the *Zürichsee Zeitung*, 7 December 1938.

3

'THE EXPERIMENT MUST BE MADE'

It is commonly believed that after his break with Freud, Jung was completely isolated and abandoned by his former colleagues. The mythologisation of the Freud–Jung break obscures the extent to which what occurred was the institutional separation of the Zurich Psychoanalytical Association from the IPA. Nor was this all. A critical event during this period which is generally overlooked was the separation of the Zurich Psychoanalytical Association from the Burghölzli – the psychiatric clinic of the University of Zurich. It was this event that led to psychoanalysis and analytical psychology developing in Zurich under the auspices of their own institutions.

Whilst a number of individuals whom Jung had introduced to psychoanalysis remained loyal to Freud, this was not the case in Zurich itself.[1] Some indication of the level of public interest in psychoanalysis in this period is provided by the fact that a lecture which Jung gave in Zurich on 20 January 1912 was attended by approximately 600 people.[2]

On 10 July 1914 the Zurich Psychoanalytic Association took a decision by a vote of fifteen to one to leave the IPA. Shortly after, Ludwig Binswanger wrote about this decision to Freud:

> You will have heard that the Zurich group has decided to resign from the International psychoanalytical association with 15 votes against 1. Whether this vote was mine or not I do not know, because I was not present at the particular

---

1 An example of someone whom Jung had analysed and introduced to psychoanalysis who remained loyal to Freud was A. W. Van Renterghem. See my 'Two unknown early cases of Jung'.

2 *Zentralblatt für Psychoanalyse* 2, 1912, p. 480.

meeting, but had only explained telephonically to Maeder beforehand that I would vote against a separation. I can accept neither the latent nor the manifest reason for a detachment. I find it especially amusing that the endangering of free research was also used here as a terrible spectre. I cannot agree to further work in common with the new independent association and am quite ready to join the Vienna or Berlin group, if you advise me to; I don't know how you yourself consider the further survival of the International association, since Jung has so disappointed your hopes.[3]

This meeting took place after the appearance of Freud's denunciation of Jung and the Zurich school in his 'On the history of the psycho-analytic movement', in which he announced Jung's secession from the movement and contended that Jung's work should no longer be called psychoanalysis. In the minutes of the Zurich Psychoanalytic Association the reasons given for the secession was that Freud had established an orthodoxy which impeded free and independent research.[4] Jung informed his colleague Poul Bjerre that after Freud's 'On the history of the psycho-analytic movement', in which he clearly bases ψa on the principle of authority', Maeder proposed that the Zurich group resign *en masse*.[5] At a later meeting on 30 October it was decided to rename the society the Association for Analytical Psychology on the suggestion of Professor Messmer. From the evidence of its minutes, this society remained in existence at least until 1918 and was a professional body of analysts, most of whom were medical doctors. The reasons given for the separation of the Zurich group from the IPA indicate the principles by which it intended to organise itself: freedom from dogmatism and from the

3 Bingswanger to Freud, 22 July 1914, *Sigmund freud Ludwig Bingswanger Briefwechsel 1908–1939*, p. 141. From an examination of the minutes of the Zurich Psychoanalytic Association, it appears that the one dissenting vote recorded was actually that of Frau Professor Erismann.

4 Freud had commenced his history of the psychoanalytic movement by proclaiming that 'psychoanalysis is my creation . . . no one can know better than I do what psychoanalysis is, how it differs from other ways of investigating the life of the mind, and precisely what should be called psychoanalysis and what would better be described by some other name'. ('On the history of the psycho-analytic movement', *S. E.* 14, p. 7).

5 Jung to Poul Bjerre, 17 July 1914, *Letters* 2, p. xxix.

investiture of authority in any one individual. The IPA was its counter-exemplar. The critical question was how this was to be achieved.

In Jung's life and work, the period between 1912 and 1918 was of critical importance. It was during this period, which he dubbed his confrontation with the unconscious, that he formulated his most well-known theories – of psychological types, of the archetypes and the collective unconscious, and of the process of individuation. It was precisely at this time that he began to develop what became known as Jungian analysis. In so doing, he reformulated the practice of psychotherapy. No longer simply concerned with the treatment of the sick, psychotherapy became a means of higher personality development for the healthy.[6] This was to have far-reaching consequences in the subsequent development of humanistic, transpersonal and alternative therapies and the proliferation of new soul therapies now spreading across the United States and elsewhere.

An important consequence of the reformulation of the practice of psychotherapy was its organisational implications, which led Jung to the experiment called the Psychological Club of Zurich.[7] It was actually through Edith Rockefeller McCormick (1872–1932) that the Club came about. She was the daughter of John D. Rockefeller, the founder of Standard Oil Trust. In 1895 she married Harold Fowler McCormick, heir to the International Harvester fortune. She was an ostentatious socialite and presided over Chicago high society. Her son John died of scarlet fever in 1901, after which they endowed the John Rockefeller McCormick Institute for Infectious Diseases. With her husband, she was instrumental in founding the Chicago Opera company in 1910.

Edith McCormick came to Zurich to be analysed by Jung in 1913.[8]

6 Indication of this expansion is given in Jung's introduction to *Psychologische Abhandlungen* [Psychological Treatises], a collection of papers by members of the Zurich school which he edited in 1914: 'In accordance with the character of our psychological interests, this series will include not only works in the area of psychopathology, but also investigations of a general psychological nature'. *CW* 18, § 1825.
7 On the history of the Club, see Friedel Muser, *Zur Geschichte des Psychologischen Clubs Zurich von den Anfängen bis 1928*.
8 A humorous account of her activities in Zurich was provided by her chauffeur Emile Ammann. For an excerpt dealing with her encounters with Jung and analytical psychology see Ammann's 'Driving Miss Edith'.

According to Barbara Hannah, she offered to buy a house for him in America and move him and his family over, an offer which he refused.[9] Jung once said that 'she thought she could buy everything'.[10] Edith McCormick suffered from agoraphobia, and found it difficult to travel by train. Jung suggested that she should travel by train along the Lake of Zurich, whilst being followed by her chauffeur, so she could get out at every station.[11] In Zurich, she established a fund to help impoverished artists, most prominent among whom was James Joyce. She practised some analysis and took on pupils.[12] It is reported that she thought that analytical psychology could cure tuberculosis and other diseases.[13] She also founded the Chicago Zoo in 1923.

It was through the financial gift of the McCormicks that the Club was made possible. News of its formation spread fast. In a letter to Ferenczi, Freud wryly remarked:

> Pfister writes that Rockefeller's daughter presented Jung with a gift of 360,000 francs for the construction of a casino, analytic institute, etc. So, Swiss ethics has finally its sought-after contact with American money. I think not without bitterness about the pitiful situation of the members of our Association, our difficulties with the publisher, etc.[14]

Initially, the club was housed in a sumptuous property on Löwenstrasse 1. According to her chauffeur Emile Ammann, Edith McCormick had it furnished to her taste, and employed a hostess, a

9 Barbara Hannah, *C.G. Jung: His Life and Work*, p. 109.
10 Cited by Smith Ely Jelliffe in a letter to Jung, 28 August 1932, John C. Burnham and William McGuire, *Jelliffe: American Psychoanalyst and Physician and His Correspondence with Sigmund Freud and C.G. Jung*, p. 245.
11 Barbara Hannah, *C.G. Jung: His Life and Work*, p. 110; Ammann, 'Driving Miss Edith', pp. 13–14. Hannah narrates an episode in which she unsuccessfully attempted to buy Feldbach station from the railway company to build a house there. In his version of this event, Paul Stern claims that this property was intended to house the Psychological Club (*C.G. Jung: The Haunted Prophet*, p. 149.)
12 According to Ammann, many of these were simply out to exploit her generosity, *Driving Miss Edith*, p. 15.
13 Peter Collier and David Horowitz, *The Rockefellers: An American Dynasty*, p. 73.
14 Freud to Ferenczi, 29 April 1916. *The Correspondence of Sigmund Freud and Sándor Ferenczi, Volume 2, 1914–1919*, ed. Ernst Falzeder and Eva Brabant, p. 126. I thank Ernst Falzeder for drawing this to my attention.

cook, three servants and a workman.[15] At the Club, there was a pension where paying guests stayed, a consulting room (which Jung sometimes used) and a library. Meals were served. Heinrich Steiger recalls:

> It was the idea of Mrs. McCormick to have such a Club, where one must go and have an appointment with another member for a party of billiards. Every fortnight we had a lecture on a Saturday evening, and it was possible to have a meal before the lecture. . . . So it was a possibility to come together with friends under the ideas of Jung.[16]

Thus, according to Steiger, Edith McCormick's aim in proposing the Club was to establish a place where people in Jung's circle could attend lectures, gather together socially, have meals and play billiards. Her son, Fowler McCormick, who was analysed by Jung and Toni Wolff during this period and later became a close friend of Jung, recalled:

> Father and Mother were among those, along with Dr. Jung, Mrs. Jung, and others, who formed the Psychological Club. The idea of the Club was to get people together who were interested and had been in analysis, so that they could have a social life and not just continue to be introverted by themselves, etc. I do know that Father and Mother were very instrumental in helping to get the Club started and I also remember very clearly Father feeling how little most of the members at that time (not speaking of Dr. and Mrs. Jung, and not speaking of Miss Wolff to my knowledge) knew about social life and how to have a sociable time. Father used to laugh about some of the efforts to have joyous evenings, and how they fell flat. It was all considered to be trivial and too light.[17]

---

15 Ammann, 'Driving Miss Edith', p. 15. Stern suggests that Edith McCormick proposed the Club out of homesickness: 'Perhaps in her Zurich exile Edith McCormick missed the "Saddle and Cycle", "Shore Acres", "Fortnightly", "Penman's", "Colony", and the numerous other clubs to which she belonged at home'. *C. G. Jung: The Haunted Prophet*, p. 148.
16 Steiger interview, CLM, pp. 4–5.
17 Fowler McCormick Interview, CLM, p. 59.

In these accounts, social reasons feature prominently in the rationale for the Club. If these activities are sufficient for it to be classed as a cult, there are few associations that could escape this designation.

Jung had initially invited his colleague, the psychiatrist Alphonse Maeder to be president of the Club, a position which he declined. Maeder had previously been president of the Zurich Psychoanalytic Association. He recollected,

> I said to him [Jung], 'You know, you nominate me as President, but in the background all the strings are in your hand. Only what *you* want will be done; only *you* say will be accepted!'[18]

As will become apparent, this did not turn out to be the case. Instead, Emma Jung became the first president. Barbara Hannah recalls that whilst Jung was the 'central figure and inspiration of the club', he refused to be president or to play a leading role.[19] As we shall see, it was precisely this drawing back from assuming an authoritative role which was to have profound implications for the early development of the Club and the subsequent development of analytical psychology.

Jung spoke about his aims in founding the Club on several occasions. In his foreword to Toni Wolff's *Studies in C. G. Jung's Psychology* he acknowledged her collaboration in:

> the carrying out of a 'silent experiment' in group psychology that dragged on over forty years, namely the life of the Zurich Psychological Club.
>
> This small organization of a group of thirty to seventy members which was founded in 1916, owes its existence to the unavoidable insight that individual analytical therapy (including the 'psychoanalytic' method) represents a dialectical process passing between two individuals, and therefore guarantees only a one-sided result from the collective-social point of view . . . in the group, namely all those events occur

18 Alphonse Maeder interview, CLM, pp. 6–7.
19 Barbara Hannah, *C. G. Jung: His Life and Work*, p. 131.

which are never constellated by an individual, or can even be unintentionally suppressed.[20]

Noll cites the first sentence of this statement, but not the remainder. This omission is not insignificant. To argue with any cogency that through founding the Club, Jung founded a charismatic cult centred around his own person of middle-class neopagan sun worshippers, it would be necessary to take into account all of Jung's professed reasons for the founding the Club and either show how they amounted to the founding of such a cult or give due reason for discounting them. In this instance, Jung gave strictly psychological reasons for the founding of the Club: to overcome the limitations imposed by one-to-one analysis. This would be frequently reiterated later by proponents of so-called group therapy. What is highly significant about this statement is that the same point was made by Jung on other occasions.

The first is a previously unpublished prefatory note to Jung's paper 'Individuation and collectivity', which he delivered to the Club in October 1916. The second is an undated letter written by Jung around 1918 to his colleague Alphonse Maeder, at a moment of ongoing difficulties in the Club. Given their temporal proximity to the founding of the Club, they are extremely important statements of its raison d'être. The first statement frames Jung's discussion of individuation and collectivity in his paper, and relates his theoretical inquiry to the function of the Club. Under the heading 'Club', he wrote:

> With this I intend the following: It is an attempt to work together as analysed men. How someone analysed reacts to someone unanalysed and vice versa is sufficiently known, but how the analysed go together is unknown. It is highly important to know this, because we must at times arrange our practical analysis in consequence of this. We are acquainted in analysis up till now only with the function of the personal-collective (analyst and patient), just as we have learnt much about the individual function. But we know nothing about the collective function of individuals and its conditions. Because of this one must make this practical attempt, because no other possibilities to have this experience are present.[21]

---

20 Jung, foreword to Toni Wolff's *Studies in Jungian Psychology*, *CW* 18, § 888–9, tr. mod.
21 Jung, manuscript of 'Individuation and collectivity', ©Erbengemeinschaft, C. G. Jung (hereafter EJ) (original in German).

The consistency of conception and expression in Jung's statements about the Club is highly striking. To Alphonse Maeder, he wrote:

> The Club is really originally an idea of Mrs. McCormick. Without the participation of her idea, she would not have condescended so far to our favours. If she had given the same possibilities into my hands completely unconditionally, I would have naturally asked all of you what should be done. I secured the cause with much work, so that at the end of a period of two years we have our hands completely free and can do what we want. I agreed with the idea of the Club, because it seemed to us to be of the greatest importance to experience how analysed people met together without compulsion, and where the flaws in our analysis of the collective function lay. I have up till now learnt an extraordinary amount in the Club. *The experiment must be made.* As I've said, we will be free in the future. By then, I hope, my friends will also have found speech. *I am absolutely prepared, in every respect, to withdraw and leave others a free path.*[22]

In this letter to Maeder, Jung states that the Club was originally Edith McCormick's idea, and that it was only after much struggle that it had obtained its independence. His conception of the aims of the Club is clearly stated: 'to experience how analysed people met together without compulsion, and where the flaws in our analysis of the collective function lay'. Maeder was one of Jung's closest colleagues, and his first choice as president of the Club. On what grounds should one doubt that the reasons Jung gave him for the founding of the Club – which correspond to his subsequent published statement cited above – were the real ones? Jung's desire to see how analysed individuals interacted was in keeping with his extension of the practice of psychotherapy to encompass higher development. It can also be read as a novel means of conducting an outcome study: realising the limitations of the effects of analysis through observing the post-analytic conduct of patients.

22 Jung to Maeder, EJ, (original in German). The letter has a handwritten note on the top, 'after 1918'. This date may have been arrived at from Jung's reference to the two years that had elapsed since the founding of the Club. The emphasis is in the original.

Another statement occurs in the transcripts of Jung's interviews with Aniela Jaffé, which were not included in *Memories, Dreams, Reflections*. According to Jaffé, Jung recalled that at the beginning of his practice transference was a major issue, and he had many cases with difficult transferences. His patients needed to adapt to society, to be together with others in similar situations, and to learn social responsibility. This led him to found the Club, which proved to be a strenuous task.[23] Given Jung's aims indicated above, it makes perfect sense that in 1916 he should be talking to the Club on the relation of the individual to collectivity.[24]

From these statements, one can deduce that for Jung, the aim of the Club was precisely to study the relation of individuals to the group, and to provide a naturalistic setting for psychological observation which overcame the limitations of one-to-one analysis. One may speculate that this was necessary because during this period, as mentioned earlier, Jung sought to shift from a pathological psychology to a general psychology of the 'healthy'. This extension occurred through Jung's work on psychological types, which was the topic upon which he was engaged during this period. Let us recall that in 1913, when Jung presented his paper on psychological types at the psychoanalytic congress in Munich, there were just two types: the introvert characterised by thinking, and the extravert characterised

23 Jung/Jaffé protocols, Library of Congress, p. 321. Barbara Hannah provides the following account of the genesis and raison d'être of the Club, which echoes and amplifies Jung's statements: 'As the group around him increased, it became a problem how to give it some corporate life. For the most part the individuals of the group did not even know each other. They were mainly, though not entirely, pupils and patients of Jung, but they naturally never met, except occasionally in his waiting room. Nevertheless they were joined together in the unconscious by their common interest in psychology. Jung increasingly felt that they needed a social group as a *reality* basis for what they were learning in psychology . . . he began to feel the need for opportunities to get to know his patients and their reactions in a setting nearer to outer life than the consulting room and the analytical hour. He often felt that he could learn much more about certain aspects of his patients by seeing them in a group than by what they told him during their hours. . . . The need to find some kind of social group or life for his patients was entirely in order to prevent them getting too isolated and cut off from life. . . . The people in analysis badly needed a place where they were not alone but could meet other people with the same interests, where they could exchange views and find companionship. He also arranged for lectures on psychology and kindred subjects and encouraged his pupils and patients to try out their own ability to lecture'. *C. G. Jung: His Life and Work*, p. 130.
24 Jung, 'Adaptation, individuation, collectivity', *CW* 18.

by feeling. By the time Jung published *Psychological Types* in 1921, this model had expanded to encompass two main attitude types of introverts and extroverts further subdivided by the predominance of one of the four psychological functions of thinking, feeling, sensation and intuition. It seems reasonable to infer that the Club was one of the main arenas of observation for Jung in the development of his typology, and his understanding of the interrelations between individuals of different types. Significantly enough in this respect, Jung read drafts of his work on types to the Club. If the Club for Jung was an experiment that had to be made, its outcome and enduring legacy was *Psychological Types*.

4

THE TRIBUNAL

In the last chapter, we examined Jung's professed psychological aims in founding the Club, which there is no plausible reason to doubt, and noted their coherence in the context of some of the key theoretical issues with which he was engaged during this period. It is time now to return to Noll's account.

Noll claims that the Club constituted the governing organ of the spiritual elite constituted by patients and analysts who 'blurred the boundaries of their relationships'. It is somewhat anachronistic to speak of 'blurring boundaries' when current conceptions of the sacrosanct nature of analytical boundaries had not been established, and furthermore, were never avowed by Jung. Noll then adds that 'we have what appears to be a summary transcript of the talk' that Jung gave at the inaugural meeting of the Club.[1] This, he claims is 'probably an original English transcription typed by Moltzer in Zurich and, it is assumed, mailed to Katz in America'.[2] The text is untitled and consists of five typed pages of foolscap, with handwritten corrections in two different scripts. It sketches out a model of the psychological transformation of the individual, drawing on analogies from the life of Christ, Goethe's *Faust* and Wagner's *Parsifal*. From this it passes on to a description of an ideal of an analytical collectivity, and ends with practical suggestions of how the Club could be organised so as to embody this. It concludes by stating that this ideal

---

1 Noll, *The Jung Cult*, p. 250.
2 *Ibid.* As I pointed out in a letter in the *London Review of Books*, 'Why would Moltzer have done this, when at the time in question Katz's address was Bergheimstrasse 8, Zurich?' (see Appendix III, p. 107). This error of Noll's was silently corrected without acknowledgement in the paperback edition of *The Jung Cult*, p. 250.

of an analytical collectivity had been foreseen by Goethe in his poem, 'Die Geheimnisse' [The Mysteries].[3] I propose to call the text 'Analytical collectivity', as that is its main theme.

According to Noll, the meaning of this text was supposedly plain for all to see:

> It will be obvious immediately to the reader that it is spiritual redemption that is the focus of interest among this group of people and that this is not – nor was it ever – a professional psychiatric or medical association of any sort.[4]

In *The Aryan Christ*, the significance of this supposed inaugural talk is if anything amplified. According to Noll, it marked the inception of an attempt to redeem the world. Consequently analysis was transformed into a rite of initiation and patients into apostles. To convert someone became more important than to cure them.[5]

Fortunately, we do have Jung's direct and unequivocal reply to such charges. In 1956, Jung wrote to the Reverend H. L. Philp that 'The idea that I convert people, as it were to the new denomination "Jungianism" or better "Jungian Church" is sheer defamation'.[6] It would be hard to put it any plainer than that. In *Psychology and Alchemy*, Jung wrote:

> Another equally serious misunderstanding lies in imputing to psychology the intention to be a – possibly heretical – new doctrine. . . . Psychology is concerned with the act of seeing and not with the construction of new religious truths.[7]

Whose word do we trust here? The only way in which Noll's claims are sustainable is to assume that Jung is lying, completely misrepresenting his enterprise.

Noll states that what is to follow 'appears to be a summary transcription of the talk Jung gave'. A few lines later, he states that it is 'probably an original English transcription' and then that it is 'thought to be by Jung' (By whom? One may ask). At the time of his

---

3 Goethe, 'Die Geheimnisse', *Goethes Werk*, vol. 2, pp. 271–81.
4 Noll, *The Jung Cult*, p. 250.
5 Noll, *The Aryan Christ*, pp. 157–8.
6 Jung to Reverend H. L. Philp, 26 October 1956, *Letters* 2, p. 334.
7 Jung, *Psychology and Alchemy*, § 15, tr. mod.

piece in the *New York Times* cited above, Noll simply claimed that Jung 'gave a talk which formalised the founding of his cult'. Curiously, in neither place does Noll present any evidence for the fact that the text was actually by Jung, or that it constituted his inaugural address to the Psychological Club. In *The Aryan Christ* he notes that the references in the text to the forthcoming paper on the transcendent function and to the founding of the Club make it 'highly probable' that it was by Jung.[8] A massive set of assumptions seems to have been made, which until now has not met with detailed scrutiny. In *The Aryan Christ*, without providing any further evidence, Noll claims that as the audience gathered for the supposed inaugural meeting, they knew that they would be the first of a new race of spiritual saviours.[9] Nor is this all. Noll informs us that 'Jung spoke slowly, deliberately, and with great solemnity'.[10] During the course of this supposed delivery, we learn that 'All around Jung must have seen the astonished, enthralled faces of his people'.[11] Finally, at the end of Jung's supposed talk, we are told that 'The applause Jung received after this last line was well earned'.[12]

On an evidential level, there are several assertions embedded within Noll's claims: (1) that there was an inaugural address at the founding of the Psychological Club given by Jung; (2) that this was in English (if it is correct to assuming that this is what an 'original English transcription' indicates); (3) that the text was by Jung; and (4) that the text constitutes such an inaugural address. Noll does not provide evidence for any of these claims. Given this situation, one has to examine each of these in turn, and reconstruct the grounds for their plausibility.

One may begin by considering 'Analytical collectivity' and ascertaining whether there are any features which would serve to identify it as being by Jung, and by no other author. At first sight, the author does employ terms from the conceptual apparatus of analytical psychology which were developed during this period: the collective unconscious, the intuitive type, the terrible mother, the collective soul, the transcendent function. This indicates that the author was at least familiar with these terms, and had some connection with

8 Noll, *The Aryan Christ*, p. 311.
9 *Ibid.*, p. 149.
10 *Ibid.*
11 *Ibid.*
12 *Ibid.*, p. 157.

analytical psychology. Second, the author is concerned with how the Club should be organised, and expresses his or her approval of the idea of the Club, and puts forward his or her suggestions for it. This signals that the author had some connection with the Psychological Club. The first annual report of the Club shows that there were 63 members as of 28 February 1917.[13] It would thus be fairly safe to say that the name of the author is contained within this list.

At first reading, the author's highlighting of the significance of the phenomenon of deification in personality development through contact with the collective unconscious, would appear to be close to Jung's analysis in 1916 of what he termed 'godlikeness', which will be taken up in the next chapter. However, it is also possible that the author could simply have been someone who was acquainted with Jung's discussion of this theme. The account of deification, and the significance of overcoming it, may have connections with Jung's account in his 1925 seminar of a fantasy event which took place in 1913, in which he was turned into the Deus Leontocephalus.[14]

What appears to be the strongest indication that 'Analytical collectivity' is actually by Jung, and the one of two points cited in this connection by Noll, is the statement: 'I hope to elucidate this problem more fully in a work on the Transcendental Function'.[15] As is known, Jung wrote his paper on the 'Transcendent Function' in 1916, the year in which the Club was founded. This seems to be the strongest referential element. If one were to prove that someone else was the author of 'Analytical collectivity', one would have to show that this person was also working on a piece on the transcendent function.

Thus, at first reading it may be plausible that Jung was the author of 'Analytical collectivity'. Its interest would then consist in the manner in which his personal experiences, conceptual apparatus and the organization of the Club appear to be intimately linked. Needless to say, there are many other ways of understanding these connections than those proposed by Noll. However, the fact that there are features which make it plausible that it was by Jung is a far cry from establishing

13 *Jahresbericht* 1917, Psychological Club Zurich, pp. 9–10.
14 Jung, *Analytical Psychology*, pp. 95–9.
15 See below, p. 86. The 'transcendental function' was the first English translation for the term 'transzendente Funktion'. As such, it appears in Constance Long's translation of Jung's 'The psychology of the unconscious processes', p. 417. It was later replaced by the 'transcendent function'.

that it actually was by Jung, or further, that it constituted his inaugural address to the Psychological Club.

If 'Analytical collectivity' was by Jung, and of such epochal significance for the founding of analytical psychology, one would be fairly safe in expecting him to have kept a copy for himself, or for there to be a draft of some sort. However, no trace of such a text has yet been found in Jung's papers. Failing this, one would have expected a copy to be found at the Club – particularly as the manuscripts of two papers that Jung delivered to the Club were initially found there, signed and dated by Jung, October 1916.[16] These manuscripts are in German; at this stage in Jung's career, his lectures in Zurich were generally in German – this was before he commenced the practice of regularly holding seminars in English. This indicates that there is no corroboration for the fact that the text constitutes an 'original English transcription' – at best, one might say it is a translation, by an unknown hand, of unknown accuracy. In *The Aryan Christ*, Noll now states that the fact that Moltzer's name is written on it indicates that she may have been the translator, and that until further documentation emerges, he will assume that the text was a translation from Jung's German.[17] This alone calls into question any claims made on its basis. Significantly enough, no copy has been found at the Club. Given the canonical significance that Noll attributes to it as Jung's inaugural speech to his cult, ushering in a new world order of a spiritual elite, it is somewhat curious that only one copy has surfaced so far, and furthermore, in Boston.

Minutes of the Psychological Club do exist, including that of the first meeting on 26 February 1916.[18] If the text was actually Jung's inaugural address, then the minutes should contain some indication of this.

The minutes (in German) commence by stating that 'A general meeting of the friends of the analytical-psychology movement took place, in which the psychological Club, Zurich was officially founded'. The minutes go on to note that the preparatory work for the Club had

---

16 Editorial note to Jung, 'Adaptation, individuation, collectivity', *CW* 18.

17 Noll, *The Aryan Christ*, p. 311.

18 Though he attributes such a critical significance to this event, Noll did not provide a date for it. As we shall see, the date is of importance for establishing the authorship of the text. For further information concerning the founding of the Club and some of the documents that I have cited, see Muser, *Zur Geschichte der Psychologischen Clubs Zürich von den Anfangen bis 1928*.

been conducted by Edith Rockefeller McCormick and Harold McCormick, Jung and Emma Jung, Hermann Sigg, Miss J. P. Teucher and Toni Wolff. Jung opened the meeting by reading out the deed of donation. Following this, Sigg communicated the statutes prepared by the founding committee. This was followed by a debate about the individual paragraphs, especially the third, concerning the admission of new members. It was agreed to discuss the debatable paragraphs in a smaller circle, and to revise the statutes for a second general meeting. There were forty individuals present, including twenty four women. The newly constituted Club appointed an executive committee of Emma Jung as chairman, Sigg as treasurer, Irma Oczeret as Secretary and Edith Rockefeller McCormick as the owner (Jung was an ordinary member of the Club, and never served on the executive committee).

The minutes contain no reference to an inaugural address by Jung corresponding to 'Analytical collectivity'. The bulk of the meeting appears to have consisted in the discussion of the statutes. There is no reason to doubt the authenticity of these records. On this basis, whoever 'Analytical collectivity' was by, there is sufficient indication that it did not constitute Jung's inaugural address to the Psychological Club, and neither was it delivered by anyone else on that occasion.

There is therefore clear evidence to refute Noll's claims that 'Analytical collectivity' was read by Jung at the inaugural meeting of the Club, and hence constituted the formalisation of his cult. Noll's depiction of how Jung 'spoke slowly, deliberately, and with great solemnity',[19] the supposed astonishment and enthralment of his audience and their subsequent applause, together with how Edith Rockefeller McCormick explained to her husband Jung's references to the Holy Grail and *Parsifal* on that occasion,[20] are Noll's own embellishments, without any basis in the historical record. Leaving aside the issue of an inaugural address, it might still be possible that the original statutes of the Club correspond in some way to the 'Analytical collectivity', or directly indicate that the Club was, as Noll puts it, a group of middle-class neopagan sun worshippers.

Following the first meeting of the Club, there was a second general meeting on 15 March, where revised statutes were approved. At this

19 Noll, *The Aryan Christ*, p. 149.
20 *Ibid.*, p. 227.

meeting, there were fifteen new members. The following are the
statutes of the Club, taken from the first annual report:

Statutes of the Association for Analytical Psychology[21]
(2. Edition)

1. The goal of the Association is:

    a) The cultivation and promotion of analytical
        psychology, both as a pure psychology, as well as in
        its application to medicine, pedagogy and the whole
        area of the mental sciences.
    b) The mutual support of the members in all efforts
        towards acquiring and fostering knowledge of
        analytical psychology.[22]

2   The Association has ordinary members, corresponding
    members and guests.
3. Acquiring membership is subject to the following condi-
    tions:

    a) Consent of at least 3/4 of the members present in
        the admission meeting. Secret or open choice is left
        to the respective judgement of the members present.
    b) Only those persons can come into consideration for
        membership who fulfil one of the following condi-
        tions:

        I.   At least 3/4 of the members have a sufficiently
             differentiated knowledge of analytical psycho-
             logy, whether shown through the production of
             an appropriate work or through the exercise of
             a practical analytical activity.

21 The Club was constituted as an association ('Verein') because the category of a
    club did not exist in Switzerland.
22 The goals closely resemble the aims of the IPA according to its statutes, with
    psychoanalysis replaced by analytical psychology: 'The cultivation and promotion
    of the psychoanalytic science as inaugurated by Freud, both in its form as pure
    psychology and in its application to medicine and the humanities; mutual assis-
    tance among members in their endeavours to acquire and foster psychoanalytic
    knowledge', *Freud/Jung Letters*, p. 568.

II. Someone who has completed an academic course of study with a diploma or exam.

4. Concerning the nomination of corresponding members, the discussion and resolution of the Association decides from case to case.

5. The Association grants the status of guest to persons through a possible majority decision, who comply with para 3 b)II, or who are introduced through two ordinary members.

6. The status of guest extends at most over 8 meetings.

7. Regulations for guests:

a) The occasional bringing along of guests to certain lectures is permitted to the lecturer on the prior submission of a list to the President.

b) The members occasionally have the right to bring a guest to a lecture with a prior substantiated announcement to the President.

c) The President retains the right of veto in these cases.

8. The ordinary members are obliged to attend the meetings regularly; furthermore they should participate through lectures and responses, as well as by concerning themselves with the development of the association.

a) The Secretary is to be handed an abstract of the lectures at the time.

9. The annual membership fee has to cover the following posts:

a) The hall charge;

b) the expense of the managing of the Association;

c) the cost of the library of the Association, which is respectively determined by a majority decision;

d) Unusual.

10. The Association will be annually led with a 3/4 majority in a secret vote to choose the Chairman.

11. The duties of the Chairman are:

a) Calling and directing the meeting;

b) control of the library.

12. The Chairman is given a Secretary, whose choice results from the suggestion of the President, possibly by a majority decision.

13. The duties of the Secretary are:

   a) Care of the written work of the Association, management of the protocols etc.;

14. The meetings take place in the academic semester, twice a month.

15. Altering the statutes requires a majority decision.

Zurich, July 1916.[23]

If one returns now to take another look at the text in the light of this, certain features stand out. *The proposals that the author of 'Analytical collectivity' outlines bear no relation to the actual statutes of the Club.* There is no provision for the requirement, as the author of the text states, that 'there must be in an analytical Club that perfect freedom to build an endless number of small groups'.[24] Even more to the point, the author of 'Analytical collectivity' proposes that:

From which follows that I should like to have the following principles introduced into the statutes of an analytical Club.

1. Purpose of the Club: analytical collectivity.
2. Respect for the Club as a whole.
3. Respect for the small group, as such, and ~~for the individual~~
4. Respect for the individual and his indi~~i~~vidual purpose.
5. Where difficulties arise, ~~between~~ in the Club, in the small groups or among individuals, they must be solved according to analytical principles.
6. Where insolvable difficulties arise they must be brought before an analytical tribunal.[25]

None of these proposed principles appear in the actual statutes of the Club. In the statutes there is no statement as to how difficulties are to

---

23 *Jahresbericht* 1917, Psychological Club (original in German).
24 See below, p. 88.
25 See below, *ibid.*.

be solved, nor is there any sign of an analytical tribunal. Indeed, in surveying the minutes of the Club from 1916 to 1918, there is absolutely no trace of an analytical tribunal. No evidence has yet emerged that one ever existed.

It would be highly strange if 'Analytical collectivity' was indeed Jung's inaugural address to the Club, or a text by him concerning the founding of the Club, given that nothing of what he said bore any relation to the immediate and subsequent organization of the Club. This would already make the claim that it formed a cult centred around Jung's divinity somewhat implausible, to say the least. This is particularly so given that the draft statutes presented at the first meeting were modified for the second meeting; it is hard to think that all of Jung's own suggestions would have been rejected out of hand – if he was supposedly at the epicentre of the Club, indeed, its divinity.

All the evidence indicates that this could not have been Jung's address at the founding of the Psychological Club. However, it could still be possible that 'Analytical collectivity' is a draft by Jung, written at the time of the founding of the Club, but not actually delivered, for some reason. From a comparison of its contents with the actual statutes of the Club, it is highly improbable that this was the case. To argue still that it was, would require accepting the view that Jung's recommendations had little weight in the actual setting up of the Club, which in itself would require Noll's thesis to be completely revised.

However, one may still consider Noll's claims that the Club was an organisation of middle-class neopagan sun worshippers. There is no trace of such themes in the actual statutes of the Club, which appear rather mundane and bureaucratic. Nor, for that matter, is there any reference to such activities in the minutes of the Club.

The foregoing has been sufficient to indicate the foolhardiness of basing any characterisation of the Club principally on 'Analytical collectivity'. Furthermore, if one considers the statutes of the Club, and Jung's professed reasons for founding it as outlined in the last chapter, it is evident that it was simply never intended to be a professional psychiatric or medical association. What is critical, as noted above, is that the analytical association which had gone by the name of the Association of Analytical Psychology carried on in existence, at least until 1918, and its meetings were held separately from those of the Club. The distinction between these two bodies is indicated in a letter of Jung's to his colleague Poul Bjerre of 2 April 1917 in which he wrote:

we have founded in Zurich a psychological Club with circa 60 members, in which namely the human–social side of our psychology is taken care of. In addition we have meetings of about 10 analysts which take place every 14 days, where we attempt to understand all of the great novelties which the exploration of the collective unc. has necessitated.[26]

Thus there was a group of analysts, and separately, a club consisting of analysts, ex-patients and other individuals fulfilling the membership criteria above. There is no reason to doubt the professional nature of the former group: whose aims consisted in the reformulation of medical psychology and psychiatry. It was the former which was at the centre of Jung's professional interests, and not the Club. If one does not recognise these distinctions, it is impossible to grasp the nature of these institutions.

The aims and activities of the analytic group are indicated in the following circular letter which Jung wrote on 20 April 1916:

Round letter to the analysts of the association for analytical psychology.

The separation of the former Zurich group from the International Psychoanalytical Association has led to the development of theoretical viewpoints, which up to now is not yet completed, but yet already has a series of more or less definitive results have ripened. The quick forward movement has naturally brought with it that multifarious differences of opinion and all kinds of disagreements concerning the mode of expression have developed. Although this is on the one hand an encouraging sign of mental revival, yet on the other hand very perceptible disadvantages have developed from it, namely as concerns the practical treatment of patients. It is obvious that different theoretical and terminological standpoints must lead to discussion, misunderstandings, rumours and all possible other quite useless and worthless difficulties. It is therefore in the utmost interest of our cause, if the analysts in question wanted to make the earnest attempt to establish unanimity in theoretical basic viewpoints, and

26 Jung to Poul Bjerre, 2 April 1917, EJ. Original in German.

especially in the definition and application of technical terms. Because of this I suggest to you the following, that those analysts who receive this round letter (Dr. Mäder, Dr. Schneiter, Dr. Oczeret, Dr. Riklin, Frln. M. Moltzer, Frln. T. Wolff) gather in the Club house on the Saturdays alternating with the meetings of the Association. I suggest the following procedure for the common work: for the first meeting, to which I invite you on Saturday 13 May, for each participant to bring *formulated* with them those questions which he has often wished to discuss. From the total number of the suggested themes of discussion a few will be selected as the task of the 2nd meeting. Each participant will in the meanwhile prepare for the 2nd meeting, by drawing up in a written form as good and as concisely as possible his personal views on the selected theme, and then read it in the meeting for the judgement of the gathering. In each meeting on the basis of the collective discussion which takes place a formulation of the results will be worked out, which will be entered into a protocol. This protocol should also add the judgement of the individual, in so far as this is fixed in a written form.

The demanding extra work of the individual required by this procedure is an essential contribution to the interest and the welfare of our cause, and will also redound to the advantage of each individual.

I hope for your agreeable answer.

Jung.[27]

Does this sound like a proclamation of one who is supposed to have considered himself to be the Aryan Christ? Jung's concern in this letter is with establishing a democratic form of discussion to clarify confusions and misunderstandings. The focus that he suggests on the 'definition and application of technical terms' appears to have resulted in the extensive lexicon of psychological concepts that he presented at the end of *Psychological Types*. A significant part of the period known as Jung's confrontation with the unconscious was taken up with the resolution of linguistic and terminological problems.

---

27 Jung, 'Round letter to the analysts of the association for analytical psychology', 20 April 1916, EJ. Original in German.

The distinction between the professional and the non-professional interest in analytical psychology continued throughout Jung's career. In the 1930s Jung convened a group of psychiatrists and analysts which met regularly, separately from the Club, which included Medard Boss, Hans Trüb, Wilhelm Bitter and C. A. Meier. This group held fortnightly meetings which consisted of case discussions. Boss recalled that Jung 'complained that he had no followers – no disciples – or too few disciples among medical men and he would like to have cooperation together with these few psychoanalysts in a kind of workshop'.[28]

Jung's sense of the division between the lay and professional interest in analytical psychology is reflected in a letter he wrote just after the Second World War. Replying to Michael Fordham, who had informed him that they were proceeding to form a 'medical society of analytical psychology' separate from the Analytical Psychology Club, Jung wrote:

> I quite understand that you made a separate group of the analysts. They are people who are vitally interested in psychology while the lay people often merely indulge in a sort of lazy curiosity.[29]

If one returns to the 'Analytical collectivity' and takes a close look at it, several anomalies emerge. The author of the text speaks about the intuitive type. In his published writings, this term first occurs in *Psychological Types* in 1921, where Jung credits it to Maria Moltzer.[30] In Jung's initial schema, there were just two types: the introvert, characterised by thinking, and the extravert, characterised by feeling. This same schema appears in Jung's *Psychology of the Unconscious Processes* of 1917 and is unchanged in the second edition of 1918. The preface of this work is dated December 1916. It would be highly strange, if not bizarre, for Jung to speak of the intuitive type in February 1916, when the Club was founded, and to continue utilising his twofold schema in December 1916. This indicates that if the text was by Jung, it is hard to see how it could have been written prior to December 1916. This simple fact by itself is

---

28 Medard Boss interview, CLM, pp. 3–4.
29 Jung to Michael Fordham, 14 September 1945, EJ.
30 Jung wrote: 'The credit for having discovered the existence of this type belongs to Miss M. Moltzer'. *Psychological Types*, § 773, footnote.

enough to indicate the implausibility of the text's being Jung's address at the founding of the Psychological Club. Once one has established the precise date of the founding of the Club, it only requires a quick bibliographical check to establish this telling and crucial fact.

There are three other features of the 'Analytical collectivity' that appear to be anomalous. The author refers to the 'progressive tendency of the collective soul'. Whilst Jung refers separately to the progressive tendency of the libido, and to the collective soul, as far as I am aware, this phrase does not appear elsewhere in his writings.

Further, the author of 'Analytical collectivity' refers to the fact that deification occurs through 'identification with the function of intuition, with the function of extraversion, or with the function of introversion'. In Jung's copious writings on psychological typology, I have not found the terms introversion and extraversion referred to as functions. We will return to the significance of this line later on. It is possible to suggest that this may be an error in translation, if the text is in fact a translation. But without an original, it is impossible to regard any of it as an accurate translation.

The author also refers to a work in progress on the transcendent function, which, as we have seen, Noll cites as an indication that the author was Jung. However, it is important to give the full passage:

> In studying Christ's Descent into Hell I was surprised to find how closely the tradition coincides with human experience. This problem is therefor[e] not new,– it is a problem of general mankind, and for this reason probably too, symbol- ized through Christ.
>
> I will not mention these parallels further here, as it would carry me too far from my subject, – and I hope to elucidate this problem more fully in a work on the Transcendental Function.[31]

The problem that the author intends to elucidate further in the work on the transcendent function is Christ's descent into Hell. There is absolutely no mention of anything like this in Jung's 1916 paper on the transcendent function. This makes it highly unlikely that this is the paper in question. Further, there is no other published paper by Jung during this period which mentions Christ's descent into Hell.

---

31   See below, p. 86.

According to Noll, a key indication of the *völkisch* nature of 'Analytical collectivity', and hence of the Club, was 'Jung's' proposal that Goethe's poem 'Die Geheimnisse' prophetically anticipated the ideal of analytical collectivity that 'Jung' foresaw the Club as embodying. According to Noll,

> the distinguishing features that make Jung's utopian fantasy a völkisch one are the concentrated references to core völkisch metaphors when proposing the idea of an analytical collectivity, especially its appeal as a secret, elite status. Goethe's poem *'Die Geheimnisse'* ('The Mysteries') not only conjures up images of the hierarchical ancient mystery cults of Greco-Roman antiquity (which were, partially, Goethe's models in this poem) but also to the Grail-quest imagery of an elite corps of seekers (like the heretical Templars so beloved of George) who could merge their Christian cross with Wotan's Tree.[32]

Noll adds that this poem was very popular in *völkisch* circles, and that 'Jung's' use of such a symbol was in line with other *völkisch* groups at this time. In *The Aryan Christ*, Noll adds that both Jung and his grandfather had supposedly committed this poem to their hearts. He claimed that 'Jung's' utilisation of this poem indicated a homage to his ancestors.[33] However, Jung himself had this to say about the same poem in 1921 in a footnote in *Psychological Types*, which Noll does not cite:

> Cf. Goethe's 'Geheimnisse', *Werke*, III, pp. 273–83. Here the Rosicrucian solution is attempted: the union of Dionysus and Christ, rose and cross. The poem leaves one cold. One cannot pour new wine into old bottles.[34]

One could of course view this as a deliberate ruse to throw people off the trail, but this is stretching plausibility somewhat.

If 'Analytical collectivity' was written by Jung, we have seen that it would have to have been written after December 1916, and hence would have constituted a proposed reformulation of the Club. If one

---

32 Noll, *The Jung Cult*, p. 262.
33 Noll, *The Aryan Christ*, pp. 17–18.
34 Jung, *CW* 6, § 314.

surveys the early history of the Club, there was one clear occasion where this might have taken place.

From early on in the history of the Club, there were financial problems.[35] At the same time, it was underused, and there was little participation from the members. Barbara Hannah recalls

> Toni Wolff told me it [the Club] started off on too luxurious lines, rather like an American club, and thus its restaurant and rooms proved too expensive for anyone to be able to use them![36]

The level of participation was so low that the general meeting on 19 May 1917 was the second general meeting where the statutory quorum was not reached. A circular letter on the 'Club problem' was sent round in October 1916 by Emma Jung to all the members soliciting their views on the aims and purposes of the Club, and how it should be organised. What quickly became apparent was the fact that there were not only many different conceptions of the Club, but also of what constituted its problem. The Club was in search of a clear statement of what constituted its problem. Could 'Analytical collectivity' actually have been Jung's own reply to this circular?

What is immediately clear about the replies to the Club circular is that between 1916 and 1918, nearly everyone in the Club was concerned in one way or another with its meaning and purpose. This renders Noll's claim that the fact that 'Analytical collectivity' was about the founding of the Club and therefore by Jung a much weaker argument.

What was at stake in the discussions concerning the Club problem was indicated by Harold McCormick. In his reply to Emma Jung's circular, he took up the relation of the Zurich school to the Club. Whilst these were separate entities, he claimed that the overlap of membership effectively identified them. This made the Club the 'expression of the ideas' of the Zurich school. As we shall see further on, this equation was explicitly challenged by Maria Moltzer.[37] Consequently, McCormick remarked:

---

35 For details concerning the difficulties within the Club at this period, see Muser, *Zur Geschichte des Psychologischen Clubs Zürich von den Anfängen bis 1928.*
36 Barbara Hannah, *C. G. Jung: His Life and Work*, p. 130. In 1918, the Club moved to its present abode on Gemeindestrasse.
37 See below, pp. 67–69.

It may be said with a good deal of truth that the school of Zurich is ~~somewhat~~ on trial [in so far as its] relation to the outcome of the Club enterprise [is concerned] for if 60 people in analysis cannot get along together, what can be expected for the future among 600 or 6000.

Part of the problem confronting the Club was that it was in fact a kind of umbrella, combining

a Club to be devoted to intellectual pursuits; to social pursuits, a pension; a town Club; a place for collateral society meetings; and a habitat for persons in various stages of Analysis.

It is clear that in this enumeration he does not state that the purpose of the Club was to gather together to worship the Aryan Christ known as C. G. Jung. For Harold McCormick, the Club problem consisted in the fact that the Club was not a unitary entity with a single purpose. It was an expression of different, conflicting interests.

It was the last aspect McCormick cited – the coming together of individuals in analysis – which especially created difficulties, which he diagnosed as follows:

I believe that unconsciously there is too much of atmosphere of rank observed in the Club, the mental rank, and the rank between 'analytiker' and 'analysand' on the one hand, and as between people in various stages of analysis on the other. . . . The mantle of 'caste' should be laid aside at the threshold of the Club and the Natural Simple Human Relation assumed in its real aspect.

Noll reproduced a different copy of this same letter.[38] He claimed that after a particular evening at the Club, Emma Jung saw how upset Harold was, and asked him specifically to write his views on the social problems of the Club, and how to solve them.[39]

This is completely mistaken. Emma Jung did not write to McCormick because he was upset: what he received was a circular

---

38 Noll, *The Aryan Christ*, pp. 228–9.
39 *Ibid.*

letter which she wrote to *all* members of the Club, asking for their views on the 'Club problem', and most, if not all of them, replied. Without understanding this, one completely misunderstands the context not only of McCormick's letter, but of much else also, as will become apparent.

Fortunately, Jung's own handwritten circular letter on the Club problem, addressed to the executive committee of the Club, has survived, and it is reproduced here in full in translation:

> For your enquiry, I am honoured to communicate the following as my view:
>
> The current attempt of the establishment of an analytical collectivity has up till now ripened with both positive and negative results, as was to be expected. For the future it is a matter of employing the experiences made up till now as possibly useful.
>
> As it appears to me, up to now two basic trends are to be recognized, which proceed from different principles and for that reason come to various frictions, which are certainly unpleasant for the participants, but as symptoms can be useful signposts for the future.
>
> The one tendency is characterized by a rigorous conception of the principles of analysis, whereby the so-called superficial, conventional modes of previous collectivity stand somewhat more in the background. Outwardly the rigorous, principled and individualistic thus come to a strong expression.
>
> The other tendency is characterized by the emergence of ordinary familiarity, that seeks in the Club less the rigorous application of principles, than much more a social gathering relieved of the compulsion of principles.
>
> The one tendency seeks collectivity over the analytical confrontation, the other over a presuppositionless, so to speak harmless attitude, which has simple well-being (Ghemütlichkeit) as its ground.
>
> Both are possible ways. The first way is suitable for those people who place the importance mainly on the idea of the cause, the latter for those who place the importance on their professional or civil life and for that reason do not have the same sum of libido at the disposal of the cause as the first.

If, as was frequently the case, both directions do not accord the necessary credit to the legitimacy of both ways, then personal sensitivity comes up, because one feels devalued by the other direction. This should not be. Both parties should mutually accord themselves the necessary recognition and the assurance that they are on the right way for themselves, even if their own way agrees with the other in no respect. Nevertheless the great difficulty indicated by two tendencies existing side by side should not be disregarded. Because of the extraordinarily strong collective identity which can only be dissolved through the longstanding work of self-education, one always still pulls the other down, since the one bristles against the other.

As it appears to me, for that reason in the future the possibility of a better separation of both groups should be planned, and with this the superfluous friction will be avoided. But it should not be a too far-reaching separation, since a certain measure of friction is also an element of life. Moreover certain members will at times have the need for a change of attitude, hence they must have the possibility to switch milieus.

By far the larger number of members have the need for simple conviviality as the first priority. They will thus form the actual Club.

A small number will prefer the other style. For them the idea of the pension or a home may be fitting.

Both organisations should be independent of one another in their inner regulations, so that they have the necessary freedom of their own development.

For that reason I suggest the consideration of the following ideas without obligation:

The Club could rent two suitable floors. On the upper floor the home is established. On the lower the Club locality is found, namely the library and 1–2 function rooms. Possibly catering moves into the Club from the pension. The pension is otherwise independent.

It seems to me that in this way the mutual independence and also at the same time the possibility of mutual relationship would be secured.

I yet add that the Club can only influence the pension in respect to a power of veto concerning gaining admission into the pension.

Yours faithfully,

Dr. C. G. Jung.[40]

The first thing that is obvious concerning this letter is that it is certainly not the same as 'Analytical collectivity'.[41] Second, in this letter, Jung outlines a conception of the Club at odds with that outlined in the latter. In it, he takes a somewhat cool and dispassionate view of the current conflicts of the club. These, he saw as stemming from the clash of two opposing tendencies represented by those who saw the purpose of the club as a forum for the application of analytic principles, and those who saw it as one for conviviality. Regarding both as entirely legitimate, Jung put forward practical suggestions such that these conflicts could be avoided, whilst representatives of both tendencies could remain in contact with one another.

Jung's recommendations do not contain proposals for any revision of the statutes, nor the introduction of an analytical tribunal. Clearly, they bear no relation to the modifications of the statutes proposed by the author of 'Analytical collectivity'. Further, rather than reformulating the club in conformity with analytic principles as the author desired, Jung's recommendations point in directly the opposite direction: as most members desire simple conviviality, this will 'form the actual club'.

If one is seeking to ascertain Jung's views on the purpose and significance of the Club, it is principally in his circular letter, and not in 'Analytical collectivity', that they are most clearly articulated. The contrast between Jung's circular letter concerning the Club problem and his letter to the analysts of the Association for Analytical Psychology clearly indicates the marked difference between his conception of a psychological Club and a professional grouping of analysts. To what extent subsequent Clubs and professional groupings of analysts in the Jungian world resembled Jung's conceptions, if at all, is another matter altogether.

Taking these points into consideration, the strongest indication that 'Analytical collectivity' may have been by Jung is that permission for its publication in *The Jung Cult* was given by the Jung estate.

---

40 EJ. (Original in German).
41 I have perused all of the replies and none of the replies directly corresponds to the text.

However, this should not be taken as proof of authorship, as permission was granted on the assumption that the publishers had taken sufficient measures to authenticate authorship. Therefore there exists sufficient evidence to reject beyond all reasonable doubt the claim that Jung was its author, and therefore the Noll hypothesis.

5

THE IMITATION OF CHRIST

Anyone who wishes to understand and to savour the words
of Christ to the full must try to make his whole life conform
to the pattern of Christ's life.

(Thomas À Kempis)[1]

Not only does Noll claim that Jung formed a cult, he alleges that Jung
took himself to be the Aryan Christ. These claims are intertwined. Is
there any evidence for this second claim?

In his 1925 seminar, Jung recounted a 1913 fantasy experience of
his which contained the following episode:

> Salome became very interested in me, and she assumed that I
> could cure her blindness. She began to worship me. I said,
> 'Why do you worship me?' She replied, 'You are Christ', In
> spite of my objections she maintained this. I said, 'This is
> madness', and became filled with skeptical resistance. Then I
> saw the snake approach me. She came close and began to
> encircle me and press me in her coils. The coils reached up to
> my heart. I realized as I struggled, that I had assumed the
> attitude of the Crucifixion. In the agony and the struggle, I
> sweated so profusely that the water flowed down on all sides
> of me. Then Salome rose, and she could see. While the snake
> was pressing me, I felt that my face had taken on the face of
> an animal of prey, a lion or a tiger.[2]

In commenting on this fantasy, Jung stated that Salome's worshipping

---

1 Thomas À Kempis, *The Imitation of Christ*, p. 33.
2 Jung, *Analytical Psychology*, p. 96.

of him represented 'that side of the inferior function which is surrounded by an aura of evil' and that 'this is how madness begins, this *is* madness'.[3] He went on to say that these images belonged to the ancient mysteries, in particular, those of deification: 'this was one of the most important of the mysteries; it gave the immortal value to the individual – it gave certainty of immortality. One gets a peculiar feeling through being put through such an initiation'.[4] Jung added that he had been transformed into the Deus Leontocephalus of the Mithraic mysteries. He contended that when such images arose and were not understood, 'you are in the society of the gods, or, if you will the lunatic society'.[5] It was through understanding them that their creative value could be realised.

Noll's interpretation of this fantasy plays a critical role in his work. In *The Jung Cult*, he claimed that Jung's self-deification made him the Aryan Christ,[6] a theme which is amplified in his book of the same name. He does not provide evidence that Jung ever explicitly referred to himself as the Aryan Christ. Further, he provides no cogent reasons for assuming that what Jung experienced in his 1913 fantasy, which Jung refers to in public only once, was *the* critical event that shaped his self-understanding for the rest of his life. Consequently, it is critical to try to reconstruct Jung's own mode of understanding such experiences.[7]

In 1912 Alfred Adler had stated that likening oneself to God or godlikeness (*Gottähnlichkeit*) was a motif frequently found in fantasies, fairy tales and psychoses. He viewed this as the expression of the 'masculine protest' – the desire to be a more complete man, to compensate for feelings of inferiority.[8] In 1916 Jung adopted the term to designate the feeling of universal validity which arose when an individual identified with the collective psyche, which led him to ignore the differences between people:

3 *Ibid.*, p. 97.
4 *Ibid.*, p.98.
5 *Ibid.*, p. 99.
6 Noll, *The Jung Cult*, p. 223.
7 Jung's ideas concerning religion, and particularly Christianity, underwent many shifts and transformations. For the best account of the evolution of Jung's work on Western religion, see James Heisig, *Imago Dei: A Study of C. G. Jung's Psychology of Religion*.
8 Alfred Adler, *Über den Nervösen Charakter*, p. 89.

In his identification with the collective psyche he will namely infallibly try to force the demands of his unconscious upon others, for identity with the collective psyche always brings with it a feeling of universal validity ('godlikeness') which simply ignores the differences in psychology of his fellow human beings.[9]

This led individuals to view themselves as 'the fortunate possessor of *the* great truth, which was still to be discovered, of the eschatological knowledge which means the healing of the people'.[10] Jung held that this state of godlikeness was one of the dangers of analysis, and that it represented a misunderstanding of the aims of analysis. Whilst he claimed that in any analysis that went far enough, the occurrence of such states was inevitable, the critical thing was to overcome them. The recognition of the existence of different types of human being with their own typology contributed to the overcoming of the feeling of godlikeness. Jung concluded:

In this sense analysis is no medically monopolised method, but also an art or technique or science of psychological life, which one should also continue to cultivate after the cure for one's own good and the good of the neighbourhood. If one understands it correctly, one will not set oneself up as a psychoanalytic prophet or world reformer; but, with a true understanding of the general good, one will at the outset let oneself profit by the knowledge acquired during treatment, and one's influence will have an effect more through the example of one's life than through high discourse and missionary propaganda.[11]

Thus as Jung understood it, the critical psychological task was to overcome the experience of godlikeness, and precisely not to set oneself up as a psychoanalytic prophet or world-redeemer. In his later works Jung used the term 'inflation' to refer to this phenomenon.

---

9 Jung, 'The structure of the unconscious', *CW* 7, § 460, tr. mod.
10 *Ibid.*, § 476, tr. mod.
11 *Ibid.*, § 502 tr. mod. The reference to setting oneself up as a 'psychoanalytic prophet' may be an implicit reference to Freud, in connection with Jung's letter to Freud of 18 December 1912, in which he wrote: 'For sheer obsequiousness nobody dares pluck the prophet by the beard'. *Freud/Jung Letters*, p. 535.

There are two critical features of Jung's fantasy which require explication. First, how he understood immortality, and second, how he understood the Imitation of Christ. In his paper on rebirth, Jung gives the following account of the former:

> The boding feeling of immortality which makes itself felt during the transformation is connected with the peculiar nature of the unconscious. There is namely something nonspatial and nontemporal attached to it. The empirical proof of this is found in the so-called telepathic phenomena.... The presentiment of immortality, it seems to me, is based on a peculiar *feeling of extension of space and time*. It also occurs to me that the deification rites in the mysteries were a projection of this same phenomenon of the soul.[12]

Thus far from designating a 'literal' intimation of immortality, Jung understood such experiences as arising from the projection of the nonspatial and nontemporal essence of the unconscious.

Given its significance in Christian thought, Jung had a prolonged engagement with the Imitation of Christ. A full account of this would require, amongst other things, a consideration of its significance in the history of theology together with an analysis of the problematic of imitation in Jung's work. This is beyond the current brief. However, it is important to indicate the bare bones of Jung's understanding of it. Part of the complexity of the issue arises from the fact that Jung's psychological understanding of Christianity was a component of a comparative cross-cultural phenomenology of the individuation process. This comparative perspective is frequently overlooked. Thus in his lectures on the spiritual exercises of St. Ignatius of Loyola at the Eidgenössische Technische Hochschule in 1939–40, Jung frequently drew upon parallels with Eastern conceptions to illuminate those of the West.[13]

As Jung saw it, the critical issue in understanding the Imitation of Christ was whether it was to be understood in an exterior or interior sense. In 1932 he wrote:

12 Jung, 'Concerning rebirth', *CW* 9, 1, § 249, tr. mod.
13 Jung, *Modern Psychology* 4. For an account of Jung's understanding of Eastern religions, see Harold Coward, *Jung and Eastern Thought*, and Jung's *The Psychology of Kundalini Yoga*.

We Protestants are on the best way to arrive at this problem: Are we to understand the Imitatio Christi in the sense that we should copy his life and, as it were, ape *his* stigmata; or in the deeper sense that we are to live our lives as truly as he lived his in its individual uniqueness? It is no easy matter to imitate the life of Christ, but it is unspeakably harder to live one's own life as Christ lived his.[14]

Jung urged that the Imitation of Christ be understood in this deeper sense – as opposed to the literal imitation of Christ, the attempt to live one's life as truly as Christ lived his.

A few years later, in *Psychology and Alchemy*, Jung expressed himself in stronger terms, arguing that viewing the Imitation of Christ as designating the external imitation of Christ had amounted to a 'superficial and fatal' misunderstanding:

For it is not a question of a mere imitation, which namely leaves the man unchanged and with that is merely an artifact. It is much more a matter of an involvement of the model with one's own way – *Deo concedente* – in the sphere of one's individual life.[15]

These citations have given some sense of how Jung understood the Imitation of Christ. Finally, one needs to clarify how he understood the figure of Christ. In his mature writings, Jung understood Christ to be a symbol of the archetype of the self, which constituted the totality of the psyche. Christ was far from being the only symbol of the self. According to Jung, in the East Purusha, Atman or Buddha were also symbols of the self. Here Christ is especially significant as a

---

14 Jung, 'The relation of psychotherapy to the cure of souls' *CW* 11, § 522, tr. mod. Jung expressed similar sentiments a few year years earlier in his commentary to the *Secret of the Golden Flower*: 'The *imitatio Christi* has this disadvantage: in the long run we worship as a divine example a man who embodied the deepest meaning of life, and then, out of sheer imitation, we forget to realise our own highest meaning. . . . The imitation of Christ might well be understood in a deeper sense, namely as the duty to realize one's best conviction, which is always also a complete expression of the individual temperament, with the same courage and the same self-sacrifice as Jesus did'. *CW* 13, §§ 80–1, tr. mod. See also his lectures on the spiritual exercises of St Ignatius of Loyola, *Modern Psychology* 3 and 4, p. 258.

15 Jung, *CW* 12, § 7, tr. mod.

symbol because, apart from the Buddha, he was possibly the most highly differentiated symbol of the self, and because 'he is the still living myth of our culture'.[16] In a seminar in 1939 on the spiritual exercises of St Ignatius of Loyola, Jung stated:

> The dogma claims that Christ was God who became man. In psychological terms this means that the Self approached the consciousness of man or that human consciousness began to realise the Self, as a real human fact.[17]

In a subsequent seminar, Jung simply noted that 'Christ is really the example of how a human life should be lived'.[18]

If one takes these statements together, it emerges that for Jung, the Imitation of Christ was the Western form of the 'Imitation' of the archetype of the self, so to speak. This consisted in the realisation of the self in one's own individual life – which Jung called the process of individuation.

Jung's interpretation of the Imitation of Christ is antithetical to the assumption that he believed himself to be the Aryan Christ. It may be legitimately argued that how Jung later came to understand the Imitation of Christ was not the same as how he understood it in 1913, which he would have been the first to admit. However, to write as if his putative understanding of his fantasy experience in 1913 underwent no major changes, and to completely disregard his subsequent interpretation of the Imitation of Christ, is inadmissible. If one was to suggest in all seriousness that Jung took himself to be the Aryan Christ, surely one would expect at the very least a detailed compilation and analysis of all of Jung's statements about Christ?

Noll has claimed that Jung was the most influential liar in the twentieth century. This claim seems to go beyond asserting that Jung simply misrepresented facts, and extends to stating that much of his work was simply a deception. Noll alleges that Jung used Christian metaphors to conceal the pagan nature of his thought.[19] He goes so far as to suggest that he used his research on alchemy as a facade to suggest that this his religious outlook was Christian and

---

16 *Ibid.*, § 22; *Aion, CW* 9, 2, § 69.
17 Jung, *Modern Psychology* 3 and 4, p. 201.
18 *Ibid.*, p. 257.
19 Noll, *The Aryan Christ*, p. 160.

monotheistic.[20] Such statements betray a misunderstanding of the critical significance of Christianity for Jung and consequently block any understanding of his later work.[21]

---

20 *Ibid*, p. 277.
21 To cite but one example, the interchange between Jung and Victor White, which has been excellently reconstructed by Adrian Cunningham ('Victor White, John Layard and C. G. Jung') and Ann Conrad Lammers (*In God's Shadow*), would be utterly incomprehensible from this perspective.

6

A TEXT IN SEARCH OF AN AUTHOR

If 'Analytical collectivity' was not written by Jung, who else could it have been written by? At the end of the first year of the Club there were 63 members, which leaves a rather wide choice of candidates. As the text was found in the papers of Fanny Bowditch Katz, and no other copy has yet come to light, it seems best to start with clarifying what her relation to it may have been, and indeed, whether she wrote it. To begin with, it was on the same size foolscap paper, and bore the same purple ink as another text in her papers, called 'fantasy' and dated 2 June 1916.[1] This indicates that there is a good chance that if it were not written by Bowditch Katz, the manuscript at the Countway library came from her typewriter. Ernst Falzeder notes that the use of purple carbon paper to make copies was common at that time.

Bowditch Katz was the daughter of Henry Pickering Bowditch, a famous American physiologist and friend of William James. After her father's death, she went into a depression. Her cousin, James Jackson Putnam sent her to Zurich to be analysed by Jung. In addition to treating her, Jung sent her to be analysed by his assistant, Maria Moltzer.[2] Moltzer had worked as a nurse (hence the appellation 'sister') at the Burghölzli, and became an analyst. According to Freud, Jung had an affair with Moltzer. When Jung wrote that in contrast to Freud, he had been analysed, Freud wrote to Ferenczi that:

---

1 'On this fantasy', see below, p. 63n.
2 On Bowditch Katz's analysis with Jung and Moltzer, see Eugene Taylor, 'C. G. Jung and the Boston psychopathologists 1902–1912' and my 'La folie du jour: Jung et ses cas'. In *The Aryan Christ*, Noll presents his interpretation of this episode without citing Eugene Taylor's prior and more reliable account. There is no evidence that Bowditch Katz exerted a 'long-lasting influence' on the Jungian movement, as Noll bizarrely contends (p. 166).

The master that analyzed him could only have been Fräulein Moltzer, and he is so foolish as to be proud of this work of a woman with whom he is having an affair.[3]

Moltzer worked closely with Jung as his assistant. In a letter in 1915 to Smith Ely Jelliffe, Jung described his working relation with her:

> I trusted the cases entirely to her with the only condition, that in cases of difficulties she would consult me or send the patient to me in order to be controlled by myself. But this arrangement existed in the beginning only. Later on Miss M. worked quite independently and quite efficiently. Financially she is quite independent being paid directly by her patients. . . . I arranged weekly meetings with my assistant, where everything was settled carefully and on an analytical basis.[4]

In Bowditch Katz's papers, there are diaries which contain notes of her sessions with Maria Moltzer, together with her own reflections. At times, the nature of the diary entries make it hard to separate what are Bowditch Katz's notes of Moltzer's conceptions and what are her own. This is due to the level of rapport they maintained. At one point she states that Moltzer told her that 'she had never given any other patient what she is giving me'. It also emerges that Bowditch Katz worked on copying and translating Moltzer's papers. In her diaries she uses the following terms, which indicate that she was quite conversant with Jung's terminology during this period: Abraxas, collective psyche, collective feeling, collective thinking, collective soul, collectivity, complexes, extraversion, extravert, *Gottähnlichkeit* [godlikeness], imago, impersonal unconscious, individuation, introversion, introvert, intuition, libido, Logos, persona, progressive

---

3 Freud to Ferenczi, 23 December 1912, *The Correspondence of Sigmund Freud and Sándor Ferenczi, Volume 1, 1908–1914*, p. 446. Jung's pupil Jolande Jacobi recalled, 'I heard from others, about the time before he [Jung] met Toni Wolff, that he had a love affair there in the Burghölzli with a girl – what was her name? Moltzer'. Jacobi interview, CLM, p. 110.

4 Jung to Jelliffe, late July, 1915, John C. Burnham and William McGuire, *Jelliffe: American Psychoanalyst and Physician and His Correspondence with Sigmund Freud and C. G. Jung*, p. 198.

tendency, shadow, soul, symbol, transcendent function, transcendent function of the collective psyche and unconscious. Thus she had sufficient familiarity with the language of analytical psychology to have written 'Analytical collectivity'.

At several points in her diary, Bowditch Katz takes up the relation of analysis to religion, which indicates that she was trying to work out precisely what this relation was. In one instance, she stated that analysis was religion.[5] At another juncture, on 15 July, she stated 'analysis a therapy, not a religion – but going back of Christianity, taking a more liberal view'.[6] In another place, she stated that analysis brought about a union between sex and religion, and between religion and science.[7] Her diaries present a vivid account of her inner experience in religious and specifically Christian imagery. In her own terms, she experienced a 'psychic death' in analysis.[8] She narrated the following dream:

> Dream of wound in side – my giving of my blood, i.e. helping humanity through my suffering, Christ's wound – Amfortas wishing to help humanity on the outside but not being able to – not being able to overcome the Kundry element –[9]

The likeness of the blood emerging through the wound in her side with that of Christ could be taken to designate an experience of godlikeness. The term comes up several times in her diary, indicating that it was a not uncommon ascription in Jungian circles at this time. In her reference to her psychic death, cited above, she stated 'The Gottähnlichkeit must be there – a lifting of self above life – without this man could never have been produced – this must be recognized'.[10] At another juncture, she noted: 'Van Op[huijsen]'s Gottähnlichkeit & R[udolf Katz].'s, they will fight it out!'[11] Moltzer also invoked the

---

5 Bowditch Katz 1916 diary, CLM, p. 1. These loose diary pages are numbered.

6 *Ibid.*, p. 21. Noll mistranscribes this passage to read 'Analysis is a therapy and a religion. . .' *The Aryan Christ*, p. 185.

7 Monday 7 May, Bowditch Katz 1917 diary, CLM, p. 27. This notebook is not paginated, but I have provided numbers that exactly correspond to the manuscript.

8 *Ibid.*, Friday 4 May, p. 25.

9 Bowditch Katz 1916 diary, July 10, p. 17.

10 Bowditch Katz 1917 diary, CLM, 4 May, p. 25.

11 *Ibid.*, 14 May, p. 28. Van Ophuijsen was a Freudian analyst to whom Rudolf Katz went for analysis.

term. Referring to Rudolf Katz, whom she later married, she stated that his *Gottähnlichkeit* was almost pathological.[12]

The language of psychological types enters into Bowditch Katz's diary. On one occasion early in 1917, Moltzer 'spoke of the four functions, instinct, intuition, extraversion & introversion, of realizing the soul of these functions'.[13] This is a critical statement. The author of 'Analytical collectivity' had referred to self-deification as occurring through the identification with particular functions, 'the function of intuition, with the function of extraversion, or with the function of introversion'.[14] As noted earlier, it appears that Jung never referred to extraversion or introversion as functions. According to Bowditch Katz, this appears to be Moltzer's formulation, which strongly suggests that either Moltzer or Bowditch Katz was the author, or someone else who shared Moltzer's conception of introversion and extraversion as functions.

From her diaries, it also emerges that Bowditch Katz and Moltzer both had their own conceptions of the transcendental function:

> My conception of the trans. function was not right in as much as it is a *collective* function, not an individual one. She [Moltzer] says the Logos is the outcome of the trans. function of the collective psyche and the individual element is the *consolation* of *the Logos*.
>
> The Logos is experienced through feeling but it is through *intuition* that one reaches the trans. function – and when the Logos is experienced the relation to collectivity is established – one can be quite alone but feel the bond connecting one with all.[15]

The realisation of the transcendent function played a crucial role in the development of the personality:

> *Entwicklung* [development] *and trans. function.*
> They cannot be called the same because the *Entwicklung* of the ancients meant an adaptation to God, a separation from life through an overcoming of the lower nature – whereas the

---

12 *Ibid.*, 20 July, p. 37.
13 *Ibid.*, p. 2.
14 See below, p. 85.
15 *Ibid.*, Monday 12 February, p. 3.

trans. function of today leads to an adaptation to God *and* to life. The two cannot be compared bec. the conditions are so different. In Analysis the trans. Function is used as soon as the work with the unconscious begins i.e. the freeing oneself from the Persona, getting rid of the elements which belong to the collective psyche – throwing them out into the uncon., and taking *from* the uncon. & the collective, the individual elements. Taking the valuable from Heaven and throwing the worthless into Hell. A fusion takes place out of which a new personality is created. This process goes on unconsciously and *must* be so – cannot be otherwise.[16]

Moltzer's conception of the transcendent function clearly had salvational overtones:

She had spoken of *bringing the value of the personal into the collective, of the collective into the personal.*
Her marvellously clear insight has been gained through years of labor – through trying to understand why there was so much suffering in the world and how it could be alleviated. – through the Trans. Function.[17]

Indeed, in a letter written in the first half of 1918 to Bowditch Katz, Moltzer wrote:

I'll begin with your letter of November about the transcendental funktion (sic). Through your introversion you came again in contact with the Divine, and in connection with this you realized, the transcendental funktion as the funktion by which the divine is expressed in a human form. So the transcendental funktion is the 'Mittler' [mediator] between God and Mankind.[18]

This overtly religious conception of the transcendent function was not that of Jung, who had explicitly stated that the term was not meant in any metaphysical sense:

16 *Ibid.*, Monday 26 February, pp. 10–11.
17 *Ibid.*, Monday 19 February, p. 8.
18 Moltzer to Katz, CLM. In English in the original.

Under the name of the transcendent function nothing mysterious, supernatural or metaphysical so to speak is to be understood, but a psychological function, which in its own way can be compared to a mathematical function of the same name and which is a function of imaginary and real numbers. The psychological 'transcendent function' arises from the union of *conscious* and *unconscious* contents.[19]

In *The Aryan Christ*, Noll cited the same letter by Moltzer as proof of the fact that the transcendent function was for Jung a cover name for the process of self-deification.[20] Aside from the fact that Moltzer is not speaking of 'self-deification', this conflates Moltzer's understanding of the transcendent function with Jung's, which is a mistake (the independence of Moltzer's views from Jung will become apparent in what follows).

Bowditch Katz strove to realise the transcendent function. If only she had it in her control, 'I would now, in this big account of my life, be guided by it, and would know *how* to act'.[21] As she saw it, her problem was that she had been going 'too high' to find it.[22] The key lay in the realisation that it was to be found 'through life, not life through it'.[23] The fact that both Bowditch Katz and Moltzer had their own conceptions of the transcendent function makes them both candidates for the authorship of the 'Analytical collectivity'.

One of the principal issues in Bowditch Katz's diary is that of one's relation to collectivity. At one juncture, she expressed her views on the kinds of collectivity:

Three kinds of collectivity – a Zunft [guild] or Verein [association] is also a collectivity, but on a very physical plane and usually only for eating and drinking – The Logos could never have come from such, but must come from a collectivity having a religious meaning, universal, cosmic.[24]

This indicates that Bowditch Katz was envisaging the possibility of a type of collectivity which would give rise to the Logos. Such

19 Jung, 'The transcendent function', *CW* 8, § 131, tr. mod.
20 Noll, *The Aryan Christ*, p. 196.
21 Bowditch Katz 1917 diary, 12 March, p. 13.
22 *Ibid.*, 27 July, p. 39.
23 *Ibid.*, 14 September, p. 53.
24 Bowditch Katz 1916 diary, 26 June, pp. 7–8.

reflections may well have been connected to something which she called a 'club fantasy'. Could this be the text in question? On May 18 1917, Moltzer told Bowditch Katz that her Club fantasy was very important for working out her devil, which, if she succeeded, could become valuable instead of harmful.[25] As she was developing it, Bowditch Katz gave the following description of the Club fantasy:

> Club fantasy to be worked out – the last supper developing out of the scene of revelry means finding again of that element in ~~the~~ life, the enjoyment of revelry which Christianity repressed.[26]

On 26 May, Bowditch Katz read Moltzer what she had written so far. Moltzer described it as 'splendid', and requested a copy. Bowditch Katz wrote:

> Its value lies in knowing Christ as the Mittler [Mediator], He sits on the ass and the cock is on his head – i.e. he is between the two animals; he is neither the very highest, nor the very lowest, ~~but~~ not completely God, and not completely man – but unites both, having the elements of each. The Cock is crying God of the new day, and of the Grail – Lohengrin. Although this fant. has seemed blasphemous yet I had felt none – and in writing it the lustfulness had disappeared – this because I had accepted the blasphemy which means, I had given up my old conception of religion and am creating a new. It is only blasphemous from the old point of view. This fant. is the beginning of my Bible! . . .
>
> I must carry this fantasy further – find out what Mrs McC[ormick], Miss W[olff] and Mrs Sigg mean to me – money complex, intellect complex.[27]

Thus for Bowditch Katz, the Club fantasy designated the development of her own conception of religion. As she progressed with the work, she even considered delivering it to the Club, though there is no indication that this ever took place:

25 Bowditch Katz 1917 diary, 18 May, p. 30.
26 *Ibid.*, 21 May, p. 31.
27 *Ibid.*, 26 May, pp. 32–3.

Of my reading my Club fantasy to the Club – doing it good and clearing it up. I could *only* do this if I had fully accepted the symbolic meaning in it as *in* myself – if I had done this, I could not be knocked over by anything they might say. I might be made angry but could not be knocked over, or taken off my feet.[28]

Whilst it is possible that 'Analytical collectivity' was actually Bowditch Katz's Club fantasy, the one specific element of the fantasy which she mentions, Christ sitting on the ass with the cock on his head, does not correspond to anything in the former. It may be that this was deleted at a later date, but there is no conclusive evidence linking Bowditch Katz's Club fantasy to the 'Analytical collectivity'.[29] Could it have been Bowditch Katz's reply to the questionnaire on the Club problem? This turns out not to have been the case, as Bowditch Katz wrote the following letter in reply:

My dear Mrs. Jung

In answer to your circular regarding the Club, I can only say that I very much regret being unable to give any really helpful suggestions, I *am* interested in its welfare, but until now I have not felt able to take any active part in the life there, as my Analysis has required more solitude than collectivity.

I must admit that I have felt resistances to the atmosphere at the Club, but how much of this is justified, and how much is the projection of my own condition, I am not yet able to decide. I do not yet feel ready for analytical Club-life, and is this not perhaps the state of things with many others?

Wishing you all success,

I am very sincerely yours

Fanny Bowditch

Nov 11th 1916.

28 *Ibid.*, 1 September, pp. 50–1.
29 There is another typed fantasy dated 2 June 1916 in her papers which Noll identifies with the Club fantasy which Bowditch Katz refers to here (*The Aryan Christ*, p. 182). There is no evidence that this is the case. The June fantasy, which Katz enacted, described taking three roses and laying them in an oak tree and reciting some Walt Whitman. This fantasy does not include the detail of Christ sitting on the ass with the cock on his head, nor any allusion to the Last Supper, nor anything which would specifically link it to the Club.

Bowditch Katz's inability to give suggestions, her lack of involvement in the Club and her resistances to it make it unlikely that she wrote 'Analytical collectivity' at this juncture, though these factors may have changed at a later date.

If Bowditch Katz did not write it, is there any evidence that she worshipped Jung as a divine being, in a manner befitting a member of cult? In a letter to Jung of 17 October 1917, Bowditch Katz wrote candidly of her impressions of Jung and the Club:

> A long time ago you said to me, that if a patient left Analysis with feelings of bitterness and resentment toward you, you knew there must be something wrong with his Analysis, – that remark of yours has often come to my mind of late, and it has seemed to me important for me to get back again, if possible, that good rapport which I had with you in past, but which should now be won on a much more mature basis.
>
> At that time I was still so much in unreality, and in such confusion that the real conditions of life could mean but little to me, and the transference I gave you was based almost solely on sexual excitation, – then finally came the evening at the Club, of which I spoke on Saturday, on which occasion my eyes were opened to the reality of things and I saw you in a new light, – for the first time, in the grip of your own complexes, and I realized then, and subsequently, in talking the matter over, under what stress the Club had been formed, and what a lack of harmony existed among the Zurich analysts.
>
> These things *must* reflect on the psychology of the patients Dr. Jung, and make it all the harder for them to find harmony within themselves, – for which reason it seems to be of utmost importance that such resistances as mine should be brought to headquarters, and worked out fully, even if very painful to both Analyst and patient. I cannot look at it simply as 'a fact', but rather as a situation which ought to be worked out with all sincerity and honesty, recognizing the elements of right and wrong on both sides. And it is just because you and Frl. Moltzer represent symbolically the different values which I must bring into harmony within myself, that I feel so strongly the importance of working out this piece of my development, – my Analysis could never be complete without it.

> I have read this letter to Frl. Moltzer, and am sending it to you with her consent.[30]

In this letter, Bowditch Katz's attitude to Jung is far from a blind devotion. Furthermore, it contains further indication of the lack of social cohesion of the Club. It is not clear how this episode worked out.

However, the rest is not all silence. Bowditch Katz eventually returned to America, and lived to the age of 93. After many years, she wrote a letter of condolence to Jung on hearing of Emma Jung's death:

> For a number of years now I have been working in the Arts and Crafts, specializing in Silver jewellery which I thoroughly enjoy making – especially the making of original and modern art designs – I am said to have a 'striking originality', and this, and my unusually good health for 81 years I lay to those years in Zurich. I am sure you will agree with me here.[31]

She closed her letter by expressing her 'warm appreciation of the very great help you gave me so long ago'.[32]

Thus, while there is indication in Bowditch Katz's diaries to suggest that either Moltzer or Bowditch Katz could have been the author of 'Analytical collectivity', there is absolutely no corroborative evidence to indicate that Jung was its author. As there is no conclusive evidence suggesting that Bowditch Katz was its author, and some indicating that this was unlikely, the time has come to consider the case for Moltzer as its author.

---

30 Bowditch Katz to Jung, 17 October 1916, CLM. Jung replied that he was ready to take up the work with her on his return from military duty in December. Jung to Bowditch Katz, 22 October 1916, CLM.
31 Fanny Bowditch Katz to Jung, 17 January 1956, EJ.
32 *Ibid.*

7

SISTER MARIA

Moltzer had also written a reply to the circular on the club problem, in which she criticised the current situation in the Club in no uncertain terms:

> My suggestion would be: an absolute reorganisation of the Club, since it seems to me that the present club is incurably ill.
>
> The present Club was never really a Club. Up till now it was not the expression of a Club spirit.
>
> The members of the Club should be the carriers of a Club. Up till now this was not the case. A Club that does not become financed through its members cannot live.
>
> From this it follows: that one should ask oneself once, whether an analytical Club is at all to be desired. The Club spirit should first become loud; and if it itself indicates that the Club is desirable, plans or suggestions should be developed of the manner by which a psychological Club could be founded on a healthy basis. The present members should feel it as a disgrace to be parasites.[1]

Following this, she delivered a paper before the Club in 1917 entitled, 'The relation between the Zurich school and the Club'. This paper provides the rationale for a fundamental reorganisation of the Club. As this gives an invaluable glimpse into the debates that were occurring at this time, it is reproduced in Appendix II. Furthermore, there has been a persistent and mistaken tendency to attribute all the research of

1 Original in German.

the Zurich school to the sole authorship of Jung, and not to realise the amount of collective and collaborative research which took place. In this respect, Moltzer's text stands as a valuable corrective.

Moltzer's text fuses symbolic and theoretical terms to provide a language for the transformations of inner experience. She began her paper by stating her view that an analytical collectivity could only be found amongst those who had completed their individuation, and found their way back to collectivity. Taking up the question of the relation between the Zurich school and the Club, she cited McCormick's letter, in which he had identified the two. It was precisely this equation that she questioned. As McCormick had told her that in his view, the Zurich school was identical with Jung, she then turned to Jung's letter, which should, correspondingly, answer the question concerning the relation of the Club to the Zurich school. Citing Jung's letter at length, she took up his conclusion that simple sociality was to be the basis of the Club. She raised the question as to whether this then expressed the perspective of the Zurich school. To answer this question, she turned to the issue of the theoretical rationale of the Zurich school.

According to Moltzer, the Zurich school had its commencement with Jung's *Transformations and Symbols of the Libido*. However, at present there was no agreement amongst its analysts concerning the libido theory.[2] As she saw it, the problem lay in the fact that the work in question said nothing concerning the therapeutic application of the libido theory, which still remained to be demonstrated. Leaving this issue to one side, she then argued that Jung's libido theory was incomplete, and proceeded to extend it.

Whereas Jung's work had depicted the development of the hero, Moltzer claimed that in the present time, the hero himself needed deliverance to be able to rejoin collectivity. After the fight with the terrible mother, which Jung had described, lay the fight with the terrible father, which she interpreted as consisting in an overly intellectual attitude to life. Finally, there lay the fight with the terrible child; the infantile attitude to life. What was required was for the individual to find his inner law. It was only through Christianity, she claimed, that 'the possibility of individuation [was] given to man'.[3]

---

2 If one considers this in the light of Galanter's requirement (1) for a cult – the existence of a shared belief system – it is hard to see how one can have this if there is no clear agreement on what the beliefs were.

3 See p. 96.

The conflict between the individual and the collective could only be solved with the 'greatest agony', which she saw symbolised by the crucifixion and resurrection of Christ (the author of the text had described the death of Christ as a 'death of the greatest agony'.)[4]

Like the primitives, she claimed, modern individuals also had to deify their totem (she equated this with the term imago). This process, together with the love of others and the recognition of one's individuality, led to adaptation, understanding and unity with nature. She then described the typical forms that this process took.

The giving up of exaggerated extraversion, or excessively impulsive feeling, constellated the masculine principle. The giving up of exaggerated introversion, or excessively intensive thinking, constellated the feminine principle. She argued that: 'Through the crossing of these two lines in consciousness a new principle is formed, – the principle of the child, or the Transcendental Function.'[5] A further development occurred when the child, which expressed itself in sensation or intuition, gave itself up: 'a new symbol, the symbol of the Individual Egg, appears. (Beginning of the complete transcendental function.)' This 'complete Transcendental function' she saw symbolised by the 'Divine Child or the Child of Light or the Prince of Peace, as Isaiah says, (IX. 1–6).'

At this point the conflict between the individual and collectivity is resolved, and a new harmony between 'God, man and beast' is arrived at, which is symbolised by paradise.

The process of individuation culminated in a revelation of God, which could be expressed in many different forms. Thus what needed to be added to the libido theory was the transcendent function, which she had outlined here.

Whilst the libido theory had separated itself from the older psychology, these new developments permitted a reconnection, such as encapsulated in the following statement:

> The automatisms exhaustively described by Janet, are by us turned to account, and developed into useful functions. Unconscious writing, drawing, speaking with the unconscious, and somnambulistic conditions, are for us sources of information as to what is going on in the unconscious, and in

4 See p. 85.
5 See p. 98.

this way the demons and dangers of the unconscious are overcome and controlled.[6]

After this reconnection with general psychology, it would also be possible for neurology and biology to connect with the libido theory. This was because, she claimed, there was one law operative throughout nature, represented by the libido theory and the transcendent function.

She then turned to parallels to her conceptions, which she found in Hans Schmid's article on Tristan, J. B. Lang's circular letter, and in some of Franz Riklin's paintings, which she commented on.[7] Finally, she then related these conceptions to the present situation in the Club. She pointed out that in the Club statutes, there was no mention of analysis as being the basis of the Club, and no explicit connection with the Zurich school, which led her to regard McCormick's view that they were identical as a fantasy. She recalled that:

At the founding, the guests were asked whether they could in principle accept a Club which was already made and completed, and for which Mrs. McCormick had given much money. One does not look a gift-horse in the mouth, so in principle the Club was accepted.[8]

After its foundation, she continued, the conflict between the types 'bled to death', and the problem revealed itself as being that of the relation of the individual to collectivity. Returning to Jung's letter, she stated her disagreement with his view that those who sought simple sociability would be the founders of the Club, as this attitude had to be a problem for anyone engaged with analysis. This was because it was a general wish to return to simple sociability. Those engaged in analysis find themselves alone, hence the desire for understanding company. However, for them, simple sociability risked a regression.

---

6 See p. 101. On the use of such techniques, see my 'Automatic writing and the discovery of the unconscious.'
7 Moltzer's reference to Riklin's artistic work (see p. 102) supports my hypotheses concerning the identity of Jung's 'anima voice' female patient and his colleague whom she persuaded was a misunderstood artist (see p. 16).
8 See p. 103.

A further difficulty was due to the mixing of patients and analysts in the Club. She claimed that

> a really harmless intercourse between patients and Analysts is only possible when the patient has fully developed his individuation and can therefore hold his own toward the analyst.[9]

The resistances of patients were important, and should not be overlooked, and it should be considered as valid for patients not to wish to mix with their analysts. The problem was that a 'forced harmlessness' led to an 'incestuous collectivity':

> a kind of 'Euphorie' [Euphoria], in which the person overrates himself, and imagines he has reached a phase of development which has only been stolen by way of an unconscious identification.[10]

Moltzer claimed that there should be room for different forms of sociability in the Club, which should be determined by the original groups. One of these was the pension, created for those who wished to live there; another was the home. 'The freedom to build these original groups should be accepted as one of the Club principles.'[11] She suggested that the members should meet once or twice a year for a meal to enable these original groups to form. She concluded that 'the goal of the club should be the creating of a real analytical collectivity.'[12]

Bowditch Katz's diary has already provided some evidence for the possibility of Moltzer being the author of the 'Analytical collectivity'. The fact that Bowditch Katz translated several of Moltzer's papers would account for the fact that it was in English, and that a copy of it should turn up in Bowditch Katz's papers with Moltzer's name on it.

If one turns to the 'Analytical collectivity,' one finds that the author indicated how the statutes of the Club should be reformulated to be completely in keeping with the hypothesis that Moltzer was its

9 See p. 104.
10 *Ibid.*
11 *Ibid.*
12 See p. 105.

author, as it is precisely the incompatibility of the statutes of the Club and what she sees as its purpose that she criticises. The author of the text proposed that the purpose of the Club should be: 'analytical collectivity,' which is fully in keeping with Moltzer's argument, and the contrary of Jung's. Further, the author of the text suggested that:

> So, ~~little~~ *small* Clubs will grow up in the main Club, the so-called original groups, which again have their own development to pass through, will be dissolved, or in time be change*d* into other groups. For this reason there must be in an analytical Club that perfect freedom to build an endless number of small groups, and each must respect the other. Thus the individual principle will be carried over to the collective principle, for a Club, or a small group, is, as long as it ~~consists~~ of forms a unit in itself, identical with an individuality.[13]

This is consonant with Moltzer's view that the pension and the home should be considered as original groups of the Club, and that 'The freedom to build these original groups should be accepted as one of the Club principles.'[14] This statement is almost identical to the second sentence quoted above. Significantly, there is no mention at all of original or small groups anywhere in Jung's circular letter to the Club. The author of the text indicated that they were preparing a paper on the transcendent function, and in this paper Moltzer presents her own conception of the transcendent function. The overtly religious terminology she uses to describe it differentiates her conception from Jung's, and fits in better with the connection drawn in 'Analytical collectivity' between the transcendent function and Christ's descent into Hell. The significance given to the intuitive type in 'Analytical collectivity'[15] also fits in with the hypothesis that Moltzer was its author – as it was she who introduced this concept.

Moltzer's prominence as Jung's assistant also makes it plausible that she was the author, and makes it more likely that she rather than Bowditch Katz would have written the text. Her position was such that whether or not she approved of the Club would have been seen as significant.

---

13 See p. 88.
14 See p. 104.
15 See p. 85.

Taken together, these points strongly suggest that 'Analytical collectivity' was actually written by Moltzer.[16] Whilst this is not definitively proven, the balance of the evidence clearly points in this direction. If it was not written by Moltzer, it must have been written by someone who shared her conceptions of the functions, of what was wrong with the existing statutes of the Club, of the precise ways that this should be remedied, and who had their own conception of the transcendent function. This hypothesis also has simplicity in its favour. In the Countway catalogue, the text is listed as 'Moltzer, Maria 18 – 1934? "Paper on collective element and its basis for founding a psychoanalytical club." Zurich 1913?' (However it is clear that the paper could not have been written as early as 1913, and does not concern a *psychoanalytical* Club). It is not clear who made this identification – whether it was Bowditch Katz herself, Beatrice Crossman, her executor, or a subsequent archivist. One of the ironies of this episode is that it appears that the card catalogue was correct in the first place. Thus Moltzer should henceforth be considered its author, unless any incontrovertible evidence is forthcoming that someone else actually wrote it.

Whilst Moltzer had high hopes for the Club, there is strong indication of her disappointment in it. In 1918, a year after she had presented her views on the relation of the Zurich school to the Club, Moltzer resigned from the Club. In a letter of 1 August 1918, she wrote to Bowditch Katz,

> Yes, I resigned from the Club. I could not live any longer in that atmosphere. I am glad I did. I think, that in time, when the Club really shall become something, the club shall be thankful I did. My resignation has its silent effects. Silent, for it seems that it belongs to my path, that I openly don't get the recognition or the appreciation for what I do for the development of the whole analytic movement. I always work in the dark and alone. This is my fate and must be expected.[17]

Moltzer's resignation caused consternation and led to much discussion in the Club. In June 1918, Sarah Barker, one of her analysands,

---

16 Whilst 'Analytical collectivity' reads as if it was meant to be delivered, there is no indication from the Club minutes between 1916 and 1918 that it was delivered (by Moltzer, or by anyone else).
17 Moltzer to Bowditch Katz, 1 August 1918, CLM.

presented her views on the 'Club problem' before the Club.[18] Her paper clearly demonstrates that little progress had been made from the first airing of these issues at the end of 1916. For Barker, the fact that someone of the standing of Moltzer found the Club 'so unanalytical that she could no longer give it her sanction and support' was a serious matter.[19] She argued that it was mistaken to believe, as had been asserted at the previous meeting of the Club, that 'her [Moltzer] attitude had been influenced by countless resistances brought about by her patients.'

Barker noted that from the outset, Moltzer had maintained that 'the club was not founded or conducted in accordance with analytical principles.'[20] She went to provide her own analysis of the current state of discontent in the Club, which was apparent from the lack of attendance. As she saw it, she doubted that any of the members would think that the Club could continue without the financial support of Mrs. McCormick or Jung's personal and intellectual support. This state of dependence indicated the fact that 'we have not yet reached that autonomous self-reliance which Dr. Jung and the other analysts constantly hold up as the goal.'[21] The simple recognition of this fact, she held, would serve to mitigate it.

She then addressed two criticisms which were frequently made about the atmosphere in the Club. The first was that 'the spirit of humanity was conspicuously lacking in our club life, and that in the process of reaching our individuation, the human qualities had become atrophied or killed.'[22] Whilst she did not agree with this charge, she felt that there was once some justice in it, which she encountered when she first arrived at the Club in 1916. She felt that in the pension in particular (where she stayed), much progress had been made to develop a truer conception of the principle of individuation.

The second accusation was that the attitude of certain leading members was over-intellectual, which 'created an atmosphere which crushed out all spontaneity and originality of thought and feeling.'[23] She disputed this, noting the breadth of the conversation in the Club, and the fact that 'Dr. Jung gives freely and generously from his

18 Sarah Barker, 'The Club problem'.
19 *Ibid.*, p. 1.
20 *Ibid.*, p. 2.
21 *Ibid.*
22 *Ibid.*, p. 3.
23 *Ibid.*, p. 4.

human personality, and from his inexhaustible fund of anecdote and store of knowledge and their analytical applications.'[24] However, at the same time, she felt that such criticisms indicated 'a protest from the unconscious against a tendency to adapt problems to analytical theories instead of adapting these theories to life problems, and also against an overvaluation of intellectual attainments.'[25] She outlined her hope of a possible community of analysed individuals, in which the different psychological types would all be given freedom of expression, and that the common language and shared experience of analysis would create a harmonious atmosphere. At present in the Club, this was clearly not the case, which led her to agree with Moltzer that, 'the time is not ripe for a true analytical collectivity.'[26]

If Moltzer, and not Jung, was the author of the 'Analytical collectivity', it still might be argued that owing to her closeness to him, it reflected his possibly esoteric intentions closely enough to be taken as representative of how he conceived of the Club. There are problems with this argument. To begin with, it overlooks the fact that Moltzer explicitly criticises not only the present state of the Club, but also Jung's conception of it. Her suggestions are put forward as an alternative. Second, Moltzer's proposed alterations of the statutes were never taken up by the Club, which indicates that they did not meet with general assent. Whatever the actual reasons for Moltzer's departure from the Club, it is clear from the above that she did not think that the Club was moving in the direction of her recommendations.

To read 'Analytical collectivity' in the precise historical context of the debates and circular letters concerning the Club problem that actually gave rise to it does far more to illuminate it than to fold it back into the generic and question-begging term, *völkisch*.[27] One does not even learn of the existence of these in Noll's books.

The proposals that Moltzer recommended in 'Analytical collectivity' indicate precisely the road that the Club did not go down. The division between analytical and social interests that Jung was advocating seems far more descriptive of what subsequently happened in analytical psychology: the separation of analytical groups from the

---

24 *Ibid.*
25 *Ibid.*
26 *Ibid.*, p. 5.
27 Noll's account of Jung's relation to German social and intellectual contexts will be addressed by Jay Sherry, in a forthcoming work; see his review of *The Jung Cult*, 'Case not proven.'

local clubs. Thus it is fallacious and profoundly misleading to read 'Analytical collectivity' as the original manifesto of analytical psychology, or as in any way depicting Jung's original intention. However, it is nonetheless an important and interesting text, worthy of detailed scrutiny.

Bowditch Katz and Moltzer's reformulations of analytical psychology are themselves also indicative of a wider transformation. Whilst using the language of analytical psychology, its conceptions are altered, and its aims reformulated. This is indicative of a major tendency in analytical psychology, culminating in the position today where widespread employment of Jung's conceptual terminology conceals the fact that the conceptions of psychology adopted bear increasingly small relation to Jung's.[28] This is most markedly apparent in the widespread colonisation of analytical psychology by psychoanalysis.

Far from revealing the esoteric core of analytical psychology and its societal mission, 'Analytical collectivity' is emblematic of the opposite: how some of Jung's followers have reformulated analytical psychology in a completely different direction than that envisaged by him – a process which has arguably been central to the institutional development of analytical psychology. Without this, it would not exist in its present form. The partial reconstruction developed here of the history of the founding of the Club, far from establishing a strict continuity between Jung's originary intentions and the present discipline of analytical psychology, would on the contrary serve to give some indication of the level of divergence from Jung's intentions. As time goes by, this tendency became increasingly pronounced. Analytical psychology has become a label covering a limitless variety of concepts and practices.

---

28 It is instructive in this regard to compare the agenda for further psychological research that Jung set out in his address at the founding of the Jung Institute in 1948, with what was actually carried on in analytical psychology in the half century that has elapsed since then, *CW* 18, §§ 1137–41.

8

THE CULT THAT NEVER WAS

The discussions of the Club problem indicate that there was little agreement as to the aims and functions of the Club, and indeed, of analytical psychology itself. The impression one gets is of a marked lack of social cohesion. Such was the disharmony within the Club that in 1922, Jung, together with Emma Jung and Toni Wolff, resigned from it. Two years later they returned.[1] On this level alone, the Club clearly does not fulfil criteria (2) of the requirements of a cult cited by Noll: 'A high level of *social cohesiveness*'.[2] As a result of these discussions, two committees were set up, one to deal with entertainment, and the other with intellectual programmes. Sociable evenings with music and dancing were introduced. (Fowler McCormick's recollections cited earlier give some indication of the 'success' of these evenings.) A gramophone was acquired, and a billiard table hired. In 1918, the Club moved to a less expensive residence in Gemeindestrasse, its current abode.

At the end of his chapter on the founding of the club, Noll rhetorically asks, 'why didn't we know these things about Jung before?' To this, question, he answers as follows:

No one who was in Jung's innermost circle in Küsnacht-Zurich circa 1916 has been alive for almost forty years, so we

---

1 Muser, *Zur Geschichte des Psychologischen Clubs Zürich von den Anfängen bis 1928*, pp. 6–7. There is a sense in which one can read Jung's 1925 seminar precisely as a 'return', a clarification of how he had arrived at his current conceptions.
2 In *The Aryan Christ*, Noll has now presented some material which indicates some of the disharmony in the Club. One could of course drop this clause and require less stringent criteria for an organisation to be a cult. Then again, one could simply drop the rubric altogether.

have no recorded interviews from anyone who could directly tell us what Jung said and how he behaved during this early period. . . . There were many successive generations of disciples in the Jungian camp, and the testimony of those early individuals is unfortunately lost to history.[3]

Lost to history? Not so! In this book we have already encountered interviews with Alphonse Maeder, Heinrich Steiger and Suzanne Trüb, who participated in the founding of the Club, together with contemporaneous statements of Jung concerning the aims and purposes of the Club, and some of the responses to the questionnaire on the Club problem – many more exist. This proclamation of Noll's is seriously mistaken. Were it true, there would be no way to independently confirm or deny his claims through finding corroborative or non-corroborative evidence. Fortunately, this is not the case. In *The Aryan Christ*, Noll has begun to skim the surface of the papers of some figures in Jung's circle at this time: Constance Long, Edith and Harold McCormick, without, however, formally retracting his previous statement.

One of the most pertinent statements as to the issues at hand, by another one of the original members of the Club, Emil Medtner, has actually been in the public domain for over sixty years.[4] Medtner was an important figure in the Russian symbolist movement. He arrived in Zurich in 1914, and contacted Bleuler and asked him to recommend an analyst. Bleuler gave him Jung's name. He was analysed by Jung, who also referred him for analysis to Moltzer. He was present at the inaugural meeting of the Club, and moved into the pension in the spring of 1916. He also had a close relationship with Edith Rockefeller McCormick.[5] Thus Medtner was ideally placed as a eyewitness to the founding to the Club. In his contribution to the Festschrift volume for Jung's sixtieth birthday, Medtner wrote a fascinating piece in which he detailed his contact with Jung, including his analysis. In this paper, he recalled his conversations with Jung at the time of the founding of the Psychological Club, and reflected on the nature of the organisation, and its relation to Jung:

3 Noll, *The Jung Cult*, p. 273.
4 On Medtner, see Magnus Ljunggren's *The Russian Mephisto*. This work also provides a fascinating window into some of the activities in Jung's circle and at the Club during this period.
5 *Ibid.*, p. 117.

The idea of a psychological Club is so anti-Freudian, that it should also suffice by itself as a total demarcation to differentiate the Zurich school from the Vienna school. To a typical and thereby not particularly intelligent Freudian who professes dogmatically or even fanatically to 'doing psychoanalysis happily alone' such an idea must easily appear to be mad and the Club as a madhouse. Let us ask ourselves with absolute ruthlessness, with total cynicism, both in the positive sense of autarchy and also in the negative sense of the hardness which is a characteristic of nearly every psychologist, whether there is not a kernel of truth in this last assertion? To doubt the psychological legitimacy of the founding of the Club could force us to just those individuals, who, if they have also undergone a Jungian analysis, psychologically [seelisch] belong to the Freudian species, which then breaks through unexpectedly in their demeanour. That is one more individual side of the Club danger. With the other more collective side of the danger one also thinks of a name, namely that of Rudolf Steiner. One may briefly describe this side of the Club danger as the occult-sectarian; it is also here a matter of individuals, who, completely apart from the degree of their education [Bildung] and even their analytical-psychological development actually belong to the species of European men who fill the ranks of Anthroposophy, Theosophy, Christian Science and such like. That Jung foresaw both dangerous sides goes without saying, and in addition for myself, who was present at the birth and baptism of the Club, was fully recognized from our conversations at that time (1916). That he had to fight here and had to put his patience to the test and that he eventually pacified the dangerous stirrings, should here be explicitly stated.

Through this Jung not only saved the healthy kernel of the psychological society with growth potential, but also created a close lying playground for his observations and a sounding board which appears to be suitable for the first provisional resonances to his newly emerging thoughts and experiences. It is also unnecessary to tell of all the possibilities he had given to the Club through this.

Here it is necessary to indicate Jung's characteristic, that the relation between him and the Club shows no analogies. Outsiders forgivably had no choice but to imagine this relationship only according to the analogies of an occult master, an ideological leader, a cultural club man, the director of a school or even the head doctor of an insane asylum for already convalescing neurotics. I doubt if I tried, that I could find a formulation for this quintessential unique relation between Jung's individuality and this collectivity. One can only describe this relation casuistically, drawing up the Club annals. The specific difficulty in formulating this relation lies just therein, that one has to completely leave aside the 'leadership–society' schema if one is to correctly adjust as a member of the psychological Club. With this there is yet an interrelation, that holds as an inner unwritten law in you: that what descends on you in the day, does not happen like a completely unforeseen stroke of a billiard ball. Perhaps Jung plays very good billiards: for a while he practised it fairly hard in the Club. But there were also opponents there who obtained a certain skill in this. It may be; but nevertheless what stands out in the end is the binding–nonbinding [verbindlich–unverbindliche] and natural quality of this interrelation. Because of this I would like to assert on the basis of many years of observation that the Club carries its future in itself and that it depends only so much on Jung's conscious and unconscious plans, as few spiritual mature and self conscious personalities are found together under the roof of the Club. For Jung is the first who would be pleased if it could be established that the Club, without becoming untrue to his idea as a psychological Club, did not let itself be taken in tow by him.[6]

For Medtner, the formation of a psychological Club had two dangers: on the one hand, of being a madhouse, on the other, of succumbing to 'occult-sectarian' tendencies. According to Medtner, on the basis of his contemporaneous conversations with Jung, the latter clearly saw both these dangers which he managed to pacify. For Medtner, these dangers stemmed from the personal dispositions of some individuals in Jung's circle, and not from Jung's own intentions. Consequently, Jung's relation to those around him did not fall into the model of an occult master or the head of an insane asylum. A

6 Emil Medtner, 'Bildnis der Persönlichkeit im Rahmen des gegenseitigen sich Kennenlernens', pp. 585–6.

'psychological' association, whilst bearing some resemblance to such prototypes, was singular. As Medtner indicates, it would no doubt be much simpler to subsume the new into the generic and already known, as Noll does. This is neither good history nor good psychology, for it would be to miss entirely its distinctiveness. This singularity lies in the fact that, as Jung conceived it, the Club was not intended to simply follow a particular prototype of the relation of a leader to a group, but was to become an arena in which the very psychology of such a relation could become visible and experimented with. It is clear that this project ran into serious difficulties. Nevertheless, it is critical to realise what was at stake: could there be an association of individuals, in which a consciousness of the relation could lead to a more pacific relation?[7] It is possible that Noll would say that Medtner was mistaken, or lying, and insist that Jung self-consciously founded a cult centred around his divine status. Surely we must accord more weight to Medtner's first-hand testimony than to Noll's speculations.

Noll's statement that the 'testimony of those individuals is unfortunately lost to history' is palpably wrong. At this stage in the development of Jung scholarship the foremost task is to conduct primary research to provide a firm and sound basis for evaluations, rather than to present wild speculations as facts. This holds true regardless of whether one is a proponent or critic of Jung and his psychology. Sound evaluation can only proceed by way of adequate reconstruction. To date, this has been most sorely lacking, and has enabled all manner of fantastic reinventions of Jung to gain currency. A distinctive characteristic of Jung's work is its breadth.[8] The cardinal failing of many readings of Jung is their reductive and monotonous monocausality – the nomination of one area as the key defining context for his work, to the exclusion of all others. Such readings proceed by simply ignoring or slighting large sections of it. This is a sure sign of their limitation.

7 Michael Fordham related to me that when the Society of Analytical Psychology was founded, they believed that an association of psychologically developed individuals would be better run than other associations. He stated that this did not turn out to be the case. In his view, it turned out to be worse. He said: 'It is a monster – look what it does to people'.

8 On this feature of Jung's work, see James Donat, 'Is depth psychology really deep? Reflections on the history of Jungian psychology'.

Finally, we may conclude by considering Jung's reflections on the psychology of cults, which he presented in 1928 in 'The relations between the ego and the unconscious'. Jung wrote:

I would not like to deny in general the occurrence of real prophets, but as a precaution I would first doubt each individual case, since it is too questionable a thing to casually decide to take someone for genuine without further ado. Every proper prophet strives at first manfully against the unconscious imposition of this role. When therefore a prophet emerges in no time at all, one does better to think of a psychic loss of equilibrium.

But besides the possibility of becoming a prophet, there is yet another subtler and apparently more legitimate joy, namely to become the *disciple of a prophet*. For the vast majority this is a perfectly ideal technique. Its advantages are: the 'odium dignitatis', namely the superhuman responsibility of the prophet, turns into the so much sweeter 'odium indignitatis'. One is unworthy; one modestly sits at the 'Master's feet and guards against having one's own thoughts. Mental laziness becomes a virtue; one can enjoy the sun of an at least semidivine being. The archaism and infantilism of the unconscious fantasies come completely from his account without one's own expense, since all responsibility is laid at the 'Master'. Through his deification one grows in stature, apparently without noticing it, and moreover one has the great truth – not discovered oneself – but at least received from the 'Master's' own hands. Naturally the disciples always close in together, not out of love, but for the very understandable purpose of effortlessly confirming their own convictions by engendering a collective agreement.

Now this is an identification with the collective psyche that seems altogether more advisable; another has the honour of being a prophet, and with it the dangerous responsibility. One is merely a disciple, but nonetheless a joint guardian of the great treasure which the Master raises up ... just as the prophet is a primordial image from the collective psyche, so also is the disciple of the prophet a primordial image.

In both cases inflation is brought about by the collective unconscious, and the independence of the individual suffers injury.[9]

If one is considering the subject of Jung and cults, this is possibly the most important passage in his works. It is not cited by Noll. What Jung is proposing here is *a psychology of the cult-making process*. Cults arise, according to Jung, through an identification on the part of the cult leader with the archetype of the prophet, and on the part of the follower with the archetype of the disciple. This stems from a failure to adequately come to terms with the collective unconscious. Following from this, analytical psychology, as Jung understood it, would constitute the first line of defence against cult-mindedness. If one does not accept Jung's theoretical explanation of the formation of cults through the constellation of and identification with the archetypes of the prophet and disciple, one can still appreciate the perceptiveness of his description of this process.[10]

Whether or not one finds this an adequate psychology of cults, if one wishes to evaluate any facet of Jung's work, it is essential that one has first established a comprehensive and accurate reconstruction of the facet in question. Needless to say, this holds regardless of whether one is for or against Jung. I would submit that the attempt to develop a psychology of the cult-making process requires a degree of reflective distance from this process itself, which is antithetical to forming a cult. One may contend that there are insuperable obstacles to this, that the project was a failure, or that Jung's intentions were (and continue

---

9 Jung, 'The relations between the ego and the unconscious', *CW* 7, §§ 262–5, tr. mod.

10 There is some evidence that Jung had first-hand experience with some of the casualties of such organisations. Edward Thornton, who studied with Jung, recalls a conversation with Jung in the early fifties on this theme: 'he reminded me of the innumerable *soi-disant* gurus, illuminati and such like, who had made their appearance in the Western world in recent times. Some, no doubt well meaning, had done good work, but others had not always lived up to their tradition, and had caused spiritual and psychological damage to those followers who had surrendered unquestioningly to them. They were not, however, entirely to blame for the unwarranted veneration which had been lavished upon them. Jung could speak with authority on this subject because occasionally he had come to the rescue of some of these afflicted devotees. In this connection he would quote from John 4.1. 'Do not believe every spirit, but test the spirits to see whether they come from God', *Diary of a Mystic*, p. 150.

to be) perverted into the very opposite by some of his followers – it is nevertheless critical to establish what he was attempting to do in the first place. It is quite clear from this passage that for Jung, a cult was the very antithesis of a psychological association. This constitutes a crucial negative definition of a psychological association.

In 1918 Jung stated that 'development of reactivated contents of the unconscious' at the end of the last century represented by mesmerism and spiritualism led to Anthroposophy and Theosophy on the one hand, and on the other laid the foundations for French psychopathology and especially the school of hypnotism. It was from the latter that analytical psychology emerged. He contended that it:

> seeks to grasp scientifically the phenomena of the uncon-
> scious – the same apparitions which the theosophical-gnostic
> sects made acessible to the simple-minded in the form of
> portentous mysteries.[11]

What brought analytical psychology into proximity with the theo-sophical-gnostics sects was a concern with similar phenomena; what differentiated them was their mode of approach.

Some scholars of distinction, not however known for showing any prior knowledge of Jung, have praised *The Jung Cult*, and claimed that it marks a great leap forward in Jung scholarship: 'by far the best book written on Jung to date', 'undoubtedly the best book about Jung and his movement which has yet been written', 'a highly orig-inal, daring and important contribution to Jung scholarship' and so on.[12] On the basis of this book, I beg to differ. The present book

---

11 Jung, 'On the Unconscious', *CW 10* § 21, tr. mod. The French and particularly Swiss French psychological traditions were far more important for Jung than the German *völkish* context. On this issue see John Haule, 'From somnambulism to the archetypes: the French roots of Jung's split from Freud', Eugene Taylor, 'The new Jung scholarship', my 'De Genéve à Zürich: Jung et la Suisse Romande', and my introduction to Théodore Flournoy, *From India to the Planet Mars*.

12 Quotes drawn from the blurbs on the paperback edition. At the same time, mani-fold shortcomings and errors in *The Jung Cult* have been pointed out in their reviews by scholars who have a track record in the field of Jung scholarship: Adrian Cunningham, Sheila Grimaldi-Craig, George Hogenson, Thomas Kirsch, Marilyn Nagy, Robert Segal and Jay Sherry (see Bibliography). In addition, for a critique of Noll's notion that Jung attempted to form a Nietzschean religion, see Paul Bishop, *The Dionysian Self*, p. 7, and for a critique of his general historio-graphical location of Jung, see Eugene Taylor, 'The new Jung scholarship'. Marilyn Nagy criticises Noll for failing to cite her (in my view, much more impor-tant) work and claiming a spurious priority ('The truth of the matter', pp. 25–6).

has at the same time been a treatise on method, a plea for minimal standards of scholarship, not only in Jung history, but also in its reception.[13] For without responsible and informed reception, the efforts of scholars are nullified.

On the basis of the foregoing, we have seen that no positive corroborative evidence has arisen to indicate that 'Analytical collectivity' was by Jung, and that sufficient evidence exists to refute the claim beyond all reasonable doubt that Jung was the author. Noll has accused Jung of fabricating the evidence for his theories. If what I have argued is correct, then some of Noll's own constructions are unsupported by the documentary evidence.[14] In the interests of scholarship, if anyone continues to claim that 'Analytical collectivity' was Jung's inaugural address at the founding of the Psychological Club, it is incumbent upon him or her to come up with some corroborating evidence and a reasoned refutation of the counter-evidence and arguments that are brought forward here. No other form of reply would serve to further serious scholarship. With that, I rest my case.

13 For a complementary and timely plea for minimal standards in Freud scholarship and its reception, see Richard Skues, 'The first casualty: the war over psychoanalysis and the poverty of historiography'.
14 Dinitia Smith reported that 'Mr. Noll has said that he had written to Dr. Meier and representatives of the Jung estate, asking for permission to see the notes [of Johann Honegger] .... So far, Mr. Noll said, his requests have been ignored'. ('Scholar who says Jung lied is at war with descendants', p. 9.) However, the Jung estate has issued the following rejoinder: 'So far, Dr Noll has on no occasion been denied any access to any documents by us. Furthermore, no such request for access has been submitted to us. Dr. Noll and the community of heirs have never corresponded with each other ... ' (Leo La Rosa, letter to the editor, *Journal of Analytical Psychology*.)

APPENDIX I

Frl Moltzer

In the symbol of Christ lies an identification of the personality with the progressive tendency of the collective soul,. I purposely say the progressive tendency of the collective soul, in order to indicate that the collective soul has various aspects. One is a tendency which is represented by the Terrible Mother, but there is another which contains the symbols of redemption for suffering humanity. This side of the collective soul is symbolized by Christ.

In Christ the human and the divine in man are one, – for which reason Christ is also the God-man.

Through the death of Christ, His personality and His Imago living in mankind, became separated. Christ died, and His Imago arose among men, – and the collective soul of mankind was accepted in the symbol of Christ. Thus a new ideal arose, (appeared) an ideal so strong that its power still holds mankind today.

The identification with the progressive tendency of the collective soul is characterized by the intuitive type. This type cannot live in the existing functions, and is forced to maintain his intuition until he has found his adaptation to life. For this reason he follows mainly the progressive tendency of the libido. This identification of the personality with the collective unconscious manifests itself always in the phenomenon of self-deification, – be it an identification with the function of intuition, with the function of extraversion, or with the function of introversion. It is a self-deification according to the function, but the phenomenon remains always the same. It is therefor[e] a question of the overcoming of self-deification, which might also be compared with the Death of Christ, a death of the greatest agony.

Perhaps the freeing of the personality from the progressive tendency of the unconscious belongs to one of the most painful tasks to be accomplished on the road of development to full individuality. Through the freeing of the personality from the progressive tendency

85

arises a chaos, a darkness and doubt of all that exists, and of all that may be. The opposite tendency of the progressive is activated, and the whole Hell of the overcome past opens, and hurls itself upon the newly gained present demanding its rights, – and threatens to over-power it.

This moment brings a feeling of great danger. One is quite conscious of standing before death. The directing line, so long given one by the identification with the progressive tendency, is suddenly wiped out, – and not until one has found the continuity of the new functions created in the unconscious, can one get a feeling of the possibility to live.

The separating of the personality from the collective soul seems to disturb phylogenetically, certain pictures or formations in the uncon-scious, – a process which we still understand very little, but which needs the greatest care in the treatment. The struggle with the Dead is terrible, and I understand the instinct of mankind which protests against this great effort as long as it is possible to do so.

But we human beings have not only instinct, we have also intu-ition, – an insight into the Inexorable which life demands of us, – and so the struggle goes on between instinct and intuition, until both have been harmoniously united.

(?)Here too the parallel with Christ continues. The struggle with the Dead and the descent into Hell are unavoidable. The Dead need much patience and the greatest care,— some must be brought to eternal rest, – others have a message to bring us, for which we must prepare ourselves. These Dead need time for their highest fullfilment, – only after full duty has been done to the Dead can man return slowly to his newly created personality. This new individuality thus contains all vital elements in a new constellation.)

In studying Christ's Descent into Hell I was surprised to find how closely the tradition coincides with human experience. This problem is therefor[e] not new,— it is a problem of general mankind, and for this reason probably too, symbolized through Christ.

I will not mention these parallels further here, as it would carry me too far from my subject,— and I hope to elucidate this problem more fully in a work on the Transcendental Function. It was a problem of the past, and is a problem of our time. The night, the chaos and the despair which appear before the 'Menschwerdung' [Incarnation], has been devined by artists of not long ago. So Goethe's Faust is enveloped in night, – he becomes blind, and dies, – only then the transfiguration. The Transcendental Function which reveals the completed human being of our time.

In Wagner's Parsifal we find the same phenomenon, – only nearer to life. On Good Friday Parsifal comes back to the Gralsburg. He is entirely in black,— the symbol of death, and xxxxxxxxxx his visor is closed. The belief, in being able to fulfill the work for which he has struggled so long, has deserted him, and it is Gurnemanz and Kundry, both very much changed, who free him from his madness, and show him the way to the Gralsburg.

Only after one has freed oneself from the collective soul, only after one has passed through death, and the soul has ~~taken shape~~ been realized, ~~(only then)~~ can the collective problem be really solved. The further conclusion ~~must be~~ *is* that this problem must ~~also~~ in principle *[also]* be our problem,— the essential element in the Collective being that it pertains to all. The Collective soul may be brought to constellation in a different way in every individual, but in principle all these manifestations are ~~to~~he[1] same. When the Holy Ghost revealed Himself to the Apostles on Whitsuntide, the Apostles spoke in tongues, which means that each spoke in his own way, each had his own way of praising his own God, and yet all praised the same God.

Only after the overcoming of self-deification, only after the human being has been revealed to himself, and man recognizes the human being in mankind, can we speak of a real analytical collectivity – a collectivity which *(reaches out) extends* beyond type and sex.

But we have not yet come so far, we are on the way to the 'Menschwerdung'. The recognition and the acceptance of the personal life's task leads to the 'Menschwerdung'. The recognition that each has to fulfill his especial task, and to go his own especial way, leads to the respect for the individual and for his especial path. Only those who have been forced through their own individual law to go their own ways, and thereby *have* come into conflict with the prevailing traditions, come to Analysis.

An analytical collectivity can therefor[e] only be founded on a respect for the individual and for the individual path. The difficulties ~~in relation to collectivity~~ which arise *along* ~~from~~ the individual path *in relation to collectivity* can only be solved analytically, and it must follow that for those who wish to build up an analytical collectivity, it must be an ~~avoidable~~ *inevitable* duty to solve ~~the~~ *such* conflicts ~~arising in this collectivity, analytically~~ *according to the principles of Analysis.*

---

1 This appears to be a substitution of 'one' for 'the.'

That which those who subject themselves to Analysis have in
comm~~e~~on is their striving to solve individual problems. This mutual
interest suffices for a Club, ~~as~~ Club can be based on any one colective
element, for which reason I approve of the Club. In a Club those
persons can join together who have a common road to go, and
wherein they *thus* feel themselves strengthened in their efforts. So,
~~little~~ *small* Clubs will grow up in the main Club, the so-called original
groups, which again will have their own development to pass through,
will be dissolved, or in time be change*d* into other groups. For this
reason there must be in an analytical Club that perfect freedom to
build an endl*e*ss number of small groups, and each must respect the
other. Thus the individual principle will be carried over to the collective principle, for a Club, or a small group, is, as long as it ~~consists of~~
forms a unit in itself, identical with an individuality.

From which follows that I should like to have the following principles introduced into the statutes of an analytical Club.

1. Purpose of the Club: analytical collectivity.
2. Respect fo*r* the Club as a whole.
3. Respect for the small group, as such, ~~and for the individual~~.
4. Respect for the individual and his indi*i*vidual purpose.
5. Where difficulties arise, ~~between~~ in the Club, in the small groups
    or among individuals, they must be solved according to analyt-
    ical principles.
6. Where insolvable difficulties arise they must be brought before
    an analytical tribunal.

Nothing is new under the sun. That which I see ahead of us as an
ideal *analytical* collectivity, Goethe saw, and speaks of in his
'Geheimnissen.' If it were not so long, I should be glad to read it to
you now, – it may not be familiar to you all.

The peom was written in 1816 an*d* no doubt was far ahead of its
time. It describes a collectivity founded ~~i~~ on the principle of the religious acceptance of the individual path, and the 'Menschwerdung.'
As a symbol this Cloister has a Cross wound with roses, symbol of
the resurrted life,— the 'Tannhäuser motif' of the budding staff, the
Chider, ~~of~~ *or* the Tree of Life.

The ancients say of the Tree of Life, 'A Noble Tree *planted with*
rare skill ~~has~~ grow~~n~~s in a garden. ~~which was~~ ~~planted with rare skill~~.
Its roots reach down to the bottom of Hell, – its crown touches the
Throne of God, its wide spreading branches surround the Earth. The
Tree stands in fullest beauty and is glorious in its foliage.

This Tree is the expression of a~~n analytical~~ collection*ive* function. *Created by Analysis and life.*[2]

A note on the transcription

Words in italics indicated handwritten additions. Those struck out indicate words crossed through by hand or typed over by a row of xxx's. On close inspection, the handwriting does not match Jung's writing of this period (nor that of Emma Jung, Alphonse Maeder, Emil Medtner or Toni Wolff). It has similarities to Bowditch Katz's. The writing on the last line has similarities to Moltzer's. Spelling errors have not been corrected.

2 This last phrase is in a different handwriting.

Appendix II

THE RELATION BETWEEN THE ZURICH SCHOOL AND THE CLUB

Maria Moltzer

At our last meeting I tried to make clear to you how I had come to the conclusion that an analytical collectivity can only exist among people who, through the help of Analysis, have reached the end of their individuation, and who, from their individual standpoint, have found their relation back again to that collectivity which they had left for the sake of their individuation. At this time the very different principles of individuation and left collectivity have found a harmonious union.

Today I have to put before you the relation that exists, and that which might exist between the Zurich School and the Club.

When, in order to take part in the reorganization of the Club, I read through the correspondence placed at our disposal by the Club Vorstand [Executive committee], I discovered this problem in Mr. McCormick's letter, – which forced me to study seriously the relationship between the Zurich school and the Club.

I can perhaps assume that this letter is familiar to you, and will repeat here only the pertinent parts. 'The School of Zurich and the Psychological Club are in one way two separate propositions, but in another sense they are identical in interest, owing to the fact that the extent of membership of the Club makes this collective body almost coincident with that of the School of Zurich itself, – the Club being an expression of the ideas of the School. Therefore in a direct sense, what affects the Club affects the School and vice versa. The success of the one reflects into and makes for the success of the other, likewise the failure of the one injures the success of the other. The welfare of each is closely united in the welfare of the other. Sympathy and unity in the one means the same in and for the other.'

Here my problem is sufficiently indicated. It is: Is Mr. McCormick speaking of a fantasy or is there reality in what he writes? What is the real nature of the Zurich School and is it true that the principles of the Club coincide with it? In a discussion with Mr. McCormick, he said to me that for him the Zurich school was identical with Dr. Jung, – that Dr. Jung could exist without the Zurich School, but that the Zurich School could not exist without Dr. Jung.

After this conversation I reread Dr. Jung's letter, in which, according to Mr. McCormick, I could expect to find the solution of my problem, – as the School is identical with Dr. Jung, and the Club is the expression of the School. This letter I will also quote in part. Dr. Jung writes: 'It seems to me that there are at present two funda-mental trends expressing themselves in different principles, which, although they give rise to various frictions, and are unpleasant to those concerned, must still be considered as valuable guides for the future. One trend is characterized by a strict adherence to the princi-ples of Analysis, wherein the more or less superficial conventional customs of usual collectivity are thrust somewhat into the back-ground. Outwardly therefore the greater stress is laid on principle and on individuation.[1] The other trend is characterized by a more gener-ally human attitude, wherein the emphasis is laid less on a strict adherence to principles than on a simple, less constrained sociability. One trend is finding its collectivity through an analytical procedure, – the other, by an unprejudiced, one might say, harmless attitude, which has a simple sociability as its basis. Both are possible methods, – the first suiting those persons who lay particular stress on the conception of the idea, – and the latter, those to whom the general life-interests are most important, and who cannot therefore give the same amount of libido to the matter as the former class.'

Dr. Jung ends his letter with the remark: 'Decidedly the greater number of members feel the need of a simple sociability, and it will therefore be these who will be the real founders of the Club. A small number will prefer the other method, and for these persons the idea of the Pension or the Home would be fitting.'

According to Dr. Jung the simple sociability will be the spirit of the Club, and the question arises at once as to whether this concep-tion of Dr. Jung's is the expression of the Zurich School. In order to

---

1 This translation of Jung's letter differs stylistically from my own. In this one instance though, individuation is a mistranslation for 'Individualistische.'

answer this question, we must first realize what is to be considered by the Zurich School, – how it was formed, what it was and what is it? After Dr. Jung had written his Libido-work the Zurich School was formed. It is therefore natural that Mr. McCormick should identify the Zurich School with Dr. Jung. The Zurich School was for a long time identified with Dr. Jung, but how it is now?

In the Convent we have discovered that no unanimous conception of the Libido-theory exists among the Analysts of the Zurich School and this is not surprising. In his book, 'Wandlungen und Symbole der Libido' [Transformations and Symbols of the Libido, CW B], Dr. Jung, for the first time, defines his theory. In this notable book the theory is not developed beyond the first intuitive conception, – it contains fantasies of an unknown woman, and the proofs for the correctness of his interpretation Dr. Jung draws from all possible sources. These proofs clearly show that these fantasies are of universal value, as the conflicts expressed in them are the conflicts of all mankind.

Of the therapeutic value of the Libido-theory, this book however says nothing. The truth of the therapeutic value of the Libido-theory remains still to be proved scientifically by the Zurich School, and it seems to me that this difficult work can only be accomplished if all the Analysts will mutually demonstrate their experiences gained through the application of the Libido-theory, either in their own or in their patients' analyses.

I am sure that Dr. Jung will agree with me when I say that brilliant as the Libido-theory is, still it is not complete, as it stands in 'Wandlungen und Symbole der Libido'. To be sure the Night–sea–journey and the Sacrifice are described, and the development of the Libido is illustrated by the conception of the Hero, – but the Hero of our time has his very special duties to fulfill. The Hero of our time needs a deliverance himself.

Curious as it may sound, yet I must say that the Hero must over-come himself in order to be able to rejoin common mortals as a human being, – only by so doing can he really take part in life. As a Hero he is separated from mankind, – through the overcoming of the Hero, he again becomes one with mankind. If I had to describe the appearance of the Hero of our time, I would say: The Hero of our time is the man who, through his own individuation, has found again a harmony with his surrounding collectivity.

The Hero is a child, – that is, he who through his own nature is forced to follow his own laws is like a child. He has to travel a road that no one has travelled before him, for which reason too his difficult tasks stand as strangers before him. He is as a child because nothing already created can serve him. For this reason he has to forge his own weapons which shall meet his own particular needs. (I have a patient who had to forge three different kinds of weapons, – on her picture they are black, – but after she has learned to use them they change their color and become gold.)

The Hero has, as always, to overcome many great dangers. He has to fight the fight with the Terrible Mother, or the too impulsive extraversion, – the Night–sea–journey to the East has to be undertaken in order to free the feelings which belong to his own personality from the collective function, which latter threatens to engulf him. Through the differentiation of this function, much material is brought up from the Collective-unconscious, material which has not only personal but collective value. The separation of these values is the task of Analysis. The first process leads gradually to the personal life and the second leads back to the relation with collectivity. The patient thus finds not only his relationship to the present time but also the past, as the material produced contains not only associations with his personal past, but also reminiscences of past cultural epochs, or of human reminiscences generally, – these being probably based on his phylogenetic development.

The second fight awaiting the Hero is the fight with the Terrible Father, – (a too intellectual attitude toward life) – the fight against the prevailing opinions, against authority in general, or the collective spirit, – which must be fought through that the Hero may free his own thoughts and gain his own independent judgement.

The fight, symbolized by the Night–sea–journey to the West, is also extremely painful. The Night–sea–journey to the West, which is not described in his Libido-work, must really have been accepted by Dr. Jung as it belongs to the Libido-theory, and the accomplishment is a proof of the overcoming of prevailing opinions. The Libido-theory forces one to an analysis of the former general psychology, but even so the difficulties are not yet overcome. Beside the Terrible Mother and the Terrible Father there is still the Terrible Child.

This Terrible Child is the infantile attitude to life. The Child longs for the past, or lives in dreams of the future, because he cannot assume the responsibilities of the present moment, – so he lingers in the present situation until forced by necessity to a decision. If he wishes to be well he must accept life as it is presented to him. At the moment in which he consciously overcomes the child and becomes an adult being, – at that moment, he becomes inwardly once more a child.

He has learned to realize that he is controlled by a power which he must accept, – that he must follow a law towards which he has no responsibility, and towards which he can have none. All that can be expected of him as a human being is that he shall fulfill that which he has accepted as his life's task, and that he shall do this in a religious spirit, namely as well as it is possible for him to do it.

Expressed religiously this would mean that he has recognized the manifestation of the Inexorable God within himself, and this voice demands an unconditional obedience, – or he must suffer the consequences. Through the acceptance of the Inexorable God, the conception of the terrible God is changed to the Christian symbol of the loving and protecting Father, in as much as obedience to the inner law leads mankind to its highest perfection.

Or still differently expressed, man recognizes that he must follow the path laid out for him by the development of the Libido.

The power of life is stronger than the personal will. Life leads and must lead along paths which man not only does not, but cannot know, – and his task lies in learning to understand the laws of the libido, and in giving them practical expressions in life.

One of my patients with a strongly negative attitude to life brought me a beautiful symbol of this Terrible Child,— bringing me at the same time a picture of the Terrible Mother. In a Jewish Gnostic tradition which deals with the creation of the child, it says: 'And when the time has come for it to go forth, an angel comes to it and says, 'Go forth for the time has come for you to go out into the world', – and the child answers, 'I have already spoken to Him who spoke and created the world, and said that I am satisfied to live in the world in which I am'. And the angel answers him, – 'The world into which I bring you is beautiful, and moreover, it is against your will that you have been created within your mother's womb, and against your will you shall be born to go out into the world.' And now the child cries, – and why does it cry? Because of the world in which it was and which it must now leave behind.'

The individual of our time must come so far that he does willingly that which must be done, – and until this has been learned he will not feel free. This leads to the autonomously moral being of which Dr. Jung has already spoken in his Libido-work.

In his struggle to find his own inner law, he realizes why and wherein he differs from other individuals, and through this struggle he also learns to understand himself and finds the way in which he can join collectivity. This insight leads to a deep introversion, – an introversion which I would like to symbolize by the return to

Paradise. I did not choose this name arbitrarily, – it has arisen out of the symbols which one finds at this point of development.

Through the psychological development which mankind has passed through, feeling and thinking have separated and exist only as conflicting functions. This conflict expresses itself in personal as well as in collective life.

Faust gives expression to this personal conflict where he says:

> Du bist dir nur des einen Triebs bewußt;
> O, lerne nie den andern kennen!
> Zwei Seelen wohnen, ach! in meiner Brust,
> Die eine will sich von der andern trennen;
> Die eine hält, in derber Liebeslust,
> Sich an die Welt mit klammernden Organen;
> Die andre hebt gewaltsam sich vom Dust
> Zu den Gefilden hoher Ahnen.[2]

> [FAUST: You know one driving force,
> and may you never seek to know the other!
> Two souls, alas! reside within my breast,
> and each is eager for a separation:
> in throes with all its senses;
> the other struggles from the dust
> to rise to high ancestral spheres.[3]]

We too have experienced the collective side of this conflict in our own little circle in the question of types.

Faust is conscious of the conflict of the two functions within himself, – the type knows only the collective function in which he lives, and is antagonistic to the opposing collective function because he is not able to respond to it. One can say that the two functions have been in conflict since the time of Adam's sin, – that is, since the time that man lost part of his own soul through the 'Participation mystique' with mankind, – to use Levy-Bruhl's excellent expression.

I believe that the Totem of the Primitives or the races before Adam's time was in general an animal. The unconscious totem after Adam's time was a human being, with the enormous difference that

---

2 The transcription of these lines from *Faust* 1(1110–17) have been corrected and Stuart Atkins translation has been added in square brackets.

3 Goethe, *Faust I & II*, p. 30.

the Primitives considered their Totems holy, while after Adam's time, man despised his Totem. Man felt ashamed when they became conscious of their love, and hid themselves before their God. Then God drove them out of Paradise, and mankind lost its close relationship with nature.

In place of this he had gained his conscious understanding.

Human beings recognized their God because God had been revealed to them but they understood neither themselves nor those around them, – those with whom they were psychically united. It seems to me that the expulsion from Paradise is a gnostic representation of the creation of a continuous function of applied thinking, or of intellect, – the beginning of history in general, and the conscious acceptance of the biological function.

Only through the Christian religion is the possibility of individuation given to man, – revealed in the symbol of the child, or the divine birth of Christ among the animals. With this epoch the conscious and religious acceptance of human love begins. At the same time however, it becomes clear that the acceptance of individuation brings on a different conflict with the prevailing collectivity, and that only through the greatest agony can this problem finally be solved, – the Mystery of Christ on Golgotha and his Resurrection.

The recognition of the human Totem leads us partially back to the Primitives, – we too must deify our Totem and respect his idiosyncrasies. This deifying of the human being, the acceptance of one's own individuality and the love for another, leads to the adaptation to the present and to an understanding among men, as also to the unity with nature.

Professor Freud, who first discovered these unconscious Totems called them Father, Mother and Sexuality, and maintained that through the bondage to the [Imagos] of Father and Mother as well as to Sexuality (for the word Imago is only another name for Totem and is better suited to our time) the individual of our time is incapable of reaching a higher cultural development. This pessimistic attitude which Professor Freud expresses in his article 'Beiträge zur Psychologie des Liebeslebens' [Contributions to the psychology of the love life],[4] seems to me to be based on his lack of understanding

---

4 This eventually comprised three articles: 'A special type of object choice made by men' (1910), 'On the universal tendency to debasement in the sphere of love' (1912) and 'The taboo of virginity' (1918), *SE* 11. The first two were published in *Jahrbuch für psychanalytische und psychopathologische Forschungen*, and are presumably what Moltzer is referring to.

of the capacity of transmission of the Libido. The Libido wanders along its way over the bridge of symbols in various directions. One course leads from the concrete to the spiritual, – one from the spiritual to the concrete, and one has the tendency to expend itself in the present moment.

Thought and feeling develop with life and through symbols. There is not only a Sun-snake which carries aloft the light of conscious knowledge, – but also a Moon-snake which brings the feelings back to the soul and reveals to us the wisdom of the unconscious.

As important as the Imagos of the parents are, – however much the individual is inclined to judge the present by the past, and only with the greatest difficulty to free himself from his earliest impressions, still the development of the libido, or in other words, life, must bring him ever new impressions, ever new Imagos. The right understanding of the Imago-symbols, – of the past as well as of the present, frees the individual from this painful 'Participation mystique' which, wherever felt, must appear in the form of guilt.

Goethe praises this deliverance in Faust's glorification:

DIE VOLLENDETERN ENGEL.

Uns bleibt ein Erdenrest
Zu tragen peinlich,
Und wär er von Asbest,
Er ist nicht reinlich.
Wenn starke Geisteskraft
Die Elemente
An sich herangerafft,
Kein Engel trennte
Geeinte Zeienatur
Der innigen beiden,
Die ewige Liebe nur
Vermag's zu scheiden.[5]

[*MORE-PERFECT ANGELS.*

This remainder of earth,
it's distasteful to bear it;
even cremated,

5 Goethe, *Faust* 2, lines 11954–65. Again, transcription errors have been corrected

it would still be impure.
When a strong spirit
has taken the elements
and made them its own,
angels can't separate
two natures conjoined
in one single entity —
only Eternal Love
can disunite them.[6]]

There are two fundamentally different forms of the 'Participation mystique'. One is an unconscious identification with the external and the other, an unconscious identification with the internal elements of life. Both are unavoidable and necessary lines of development. Individuation leads the individual back further and further to his own personality. His development forces him to free himself more and more from his identification with elements foreign to himself, and to differentiate himself from the collective functions. These are not only important but most useful to him during the time of the building up of his personality, – but have now become, through his experience, development and need of independence, symbols of the Terrible Mother and the Terrible Father.

When too impulsive feeling, which expresses itself in an exaggerated extraversion, is given up, the freed libido returns to the soul from which it sprang, revives the symbols, which are the source of thought and of feeling, and brings the masculine principle to constellation, which is the principle of knowledge and of self-assertion.

When too intensive thinking, which expresses itself in a too intellectual attitude to life, is given up, and the freed libido returns to the soul from whence it sprang, it revives symbols, which are the source of feeling and of thought, and brings the feminine principle, the principle of love and of mediation (or of religion) to constellation.

The consciousness of the masculine principle leads to the tree of knowledge, – the consciousness of the feminine principle to the tree of life, – feeling as well as thinking have been again united with their origin or with their roots.

Through the crossing of these two lines in consciousness a new principle is formed, – the principle of the child, or the Transcendental

6 Goethe, *Faust I & II*, p. 301.

Function. The soul of the new individual is born, and expresses itself in the symbol of the child.

The collective functions, which before differentiation, threatened the development of the individual, now become functions which serve his development.

And when the child, the Hero, gives himself up, – the child that expresses itself in sensation (Empfindung) or intuition, and returns to the source from whence it sprang, a new symbol, the symbol of the Individual Egg, appears. (Beginning of the complete transcendental function).

Through individuation, the personal material is differentiated from the collective functions, and is enclosed in the process of individuation. This enclosing of the partial functions leads to the creation of the Individual Egg, until all four functions have been gone through, and the Hero, in order to become a human being, has to overcome himself, – now he himself slips into the Egg, – that means, he unites himself with the partial functions formed through differentiation, thereby uniting them into one single principle. Through the conscious overcoming of the child, and the conscious acceptance of the adult, the new conscious individuality, or the new human being arises, and in the soul the Divine Child or the Child of Light or the Prince of Peace, as Isaiah says, (IX. 1–6) symbol of the completed Transcendental Function is created.[7]

This function is the expression of the harmonious union of the pairs of opposites, until now having been in conflict, and from this point of view, the new adaptation to the lost collectivity is found.

This new individuality has found the harmony between God, Man and beast, – therefore the symbol of Paradise. In the symbol of the child is the indication that this function grew in a quite natural way and is the expression of life.

I said, being in harmony with God, man and beast, – in the manifestation of God in man, I wish to understand the revelation of highest knowledge, – in the symbol of the beast, the now controlled impulses, – and in that of man, the recognition of and the respect for the Self, as well as the recognition of and the respect for others, who, though different from us, are in essential point, related.

---

7 Isaiah 9, 6 reads: 'For unto us a child is born, unto us a son is given: and the government shall be upon his shoulder: and his name shall be called Wonderful, Counseller, The mighty God, The everlasting Father, The Prince of Peace.' (*The Bible*, King James Version).

In Paradise, harmony with Nature is symbolized, – or in other words, the realization that God reveals himself in the laws of Nature as well as in man and beast. Man is as much a part of Nature as either plant or beast, but the development through which man has passed has rendered him unconscious of this relationship, which he finds again through the help of Analysis.

Through differentiation from the Persona, man separates himself from the collective unconscious. In the Persona much material is brought to constellation which does not belong to the personality. The analysis of the Persona leads to the differentiation of the individual material, and to the return to the collective unconscious of those materials which do not belong to the personality. (The giving back of the feelings and thoughts which do not belong to the individuality, to the collective function, seems to me to be symbolized by the following fantasy: the spring which flows only for a certain time and must later return to the earth again, – or by the kernels, of which one does not know whether one may accept them or not and which must again return to the ancestors.)

In the personal unconscious, the opposite phenomenon is found. Here, the universal unconscious is enclosed in the personal, – as in the Persona the individual is enclosed in the universal unconscious. (The Giant and the Dwarf).

The analysis of these phenomena leads to two opposing tendencies of the libido, – one is like a materialization and leads from the spiritual to the concrete, and the other is like a dematerialization and leads from the concrete to the spiritual. Thus in the process of individuation, the tendencies (or impulses) striving towards eternity are turned around or partially forced into another direction, and a reflection of eternity passes over into man, – thus leading to the Revelation of God.

The Divine in man expresses itself in different forms, – it can be found in art, in religion, in science, in human life, in self-assertion, in love and in friendship, – elements which blend into the new individuality like the colors of a kaleidoscope.

No adaptation is possible unless one finds these elements in different variations, – at one time more love, at another time more self-assertion, a third time more friendship, a fourth time more knowledge, a fifth time more art, a sixth time more religion, is needed for adaptation. No formula can be given here, – the demands of adaptation must be ever varying, – it means an ever new effort, because it is the expression of life and life grows, passes through many different forms and passes away. Symbols of countless forms of adaptation.

What we therefore still have to add to the Libido-theory is the Transcendental Function, – and the process I have shortly outlined here. Through this work we shall prove anew the scientific and therapeutic value of the Libido-theory. It seems to me that Psychology has passed through a peculiar development by way of the Libido-theory, – it was separated for awhile from its old form and intellectual attitude in order to return again to the old lines with newly found values.

The Libido-theory has, in the course of its development, presented many difficult problems, – but, led by intuition and intellect, we have learned the difficult technicalities which enable us to give expression to the material coming from the unconscious. In this way we find a connection again with the old psychology. The automatisms exhaustively described by Janet, are by us turned to account, and developed into useful functions. Unconscious writing, drawing, speaking with the unconscious, and somnambulistic conditions, are for us sources of information as to what is going on in the unconscious, and in this way the demons and dangers of the unconscious are overcome and controlled.

It would not surprise me if, after the union with the general psychology, neurology and biology would also join forces with the Libido-theory, to their mutual advantage. Psychology has thus, in its relation to the Libido-theory, passed along the same road taken by the individual in his analytical development. Looked at from a broad point of view, one single law seems to determine the development of Nature, a law, which in psychology, is expressed by the Libido theory and the Transcendental Function.

Of course, not everyone is forced to carry through his individuation to the point of completion here described. The development of the individual is qualified by many conditions, – his disposition and the conditions in which he lived and lives will be determining factors. Each individual who learns to know the Zurich Analysis, must, at a particular stage in his development, unavoidably come to the problem of individuation. Either he will have to take the road back to colllectivity, because his gifts and powers are insufficient for the hard road to individuation, or he will find his individuation according to his own disposition and conditions. The problem of individuation is therefore for me closely associated with the Libido-theory and the Zurich school. The essential value of the Zurich school lies therefore in the recognition of the conflict between the individuation and the collective principles, and its possible harmonizing through the Transcendental Function.

When I had reached this point and formulated my own conception, I looked about and asked myself whether I stood quite alone,

– and then I discovered a number of parallel trends of thought. In order to follow them in chronological order, I would like to remind you of Dr. Schmid's article on Tristran. In this piece of work there is much which I could not agree at the time, but its essential feature lies in the conflict between the individuation and the collective principles and its possible solution through the Transcendental Function. Then I should like to refer to a few of Dr. Riklin's pictures. I hope that Dr. Riklin will not object to my considering them here only from their psychological value, – and ignoring entirely their artistic merit, – I should feel quite incapable of any other criticism.

First I should like to mention a picture which will not be familiar to you all – the first one which I saw was a representation of three red snake-like lines on a grey background. At that time I was just working on the conception of the three great sacrifices, and it seemed to me that this picture gave expression to this thought, at the same time suggesting the Transcendental reached through sacrifice, in as much as the higher and the lower are united.

As the second picture I should like to mention 'Gleichnis' [Allegory], the picture of the two curious animals, which belong not only to Heaven but to Earth as well, as they unite both, and coming from opposite directions, stand together with crossed necks, both grazing. This seems to me a representation of the two conscious functions, which have found again their soul affinity, – and in the 'Wunder' the birth of the Divine Child is revealed.

I should like also to call attention to Dr. Lang's circular letter. In the beginning of his article, he quotes from Ku Hung-Ming: 'That the cause of the European war lies in the European original sin, out of which general mistrust developed, this theory in time leading to war', and then goes on to say: 'Why has not China the theory of guilt? May it not lie in the fact that in China the collective God (Cungfutse) and the individual God (Laotse) are both recognized as equal Gods, and are not, as in the European psychology, looked on, the one as a God and the other as a Devil?' Finally Dr. Lang says: 'I feel that after individuation there should be such a Chinese world, wherein Cungfutse and Laotse reign together as principal Gods.'

For him a real analytical collectivity is not yet realizable, and his point of view here expresses my thought which I outlined in my former paper. Here also the recognition of the individual and the collective principles.

In the Zurich School the solution of this conflict between individuation and collectivity should be found. The way over the Libido-theory to the Transcendental Function is given us for this purpose.

What relation do these considerations of the Zurich School bear to what has, and is taking place at the Club? If we look at the statutes of the Club, we find nothing mentioned of Analysis as the basis of the Club. As the purpose of the Club is given: Furtherance of psychological interests and psychological science. In the statutes then, there is no connection with the Zurich School, – the Zurich School has an especial stamp that has not been accepted by the Club. I must therefore declare Mr. McCormick's conception, that the Club is the expression of the Zurich School, a fantasy. Until now the Club has not been this. The Club was an experiment. At the founding, the guests were asked whether they could in principle accept a Club which was already made and completed, and for which Mrs. McCormick had given much money. One does not look a gift-horse in the mouth, so in principle the Club was accepted.

And how was it with the Club? The fight between the types, which had begun only a short time before the founding of the Club, – was continued there until it finally bled to death, and the fundamental problem presented itself spontaneously, – namely, the relation of the individual to a given collectivity. Arrived at this point of development, the Club became chaotic and then tried to solve its own difficulties.

The rejected analytical principles once more rose to the surface and claimed recognition. They demanded their right in an analytical collectivity.

I now return once more to Dr. Jung's letter. Dr. Jung discovered two different trends in the Club, – one which tries to reach collectivity by way of analytical principles and the other which looks for a simple sociability through a harmless attitude, – and ends with the remark that the latter will be the real founders of the Club. With this conclusion, I cannot agree after the afore-mentioned point of view. It seems to me that the so-called attitude, which is based on a simple sociability must be a problem for those people who are engaged in Analysis. And why? I am convinced that it must be the general wish of all to come back to a simple sociability. The difficulty lies however in the possibility of doing this. Those who have not yet reached their individuation, or who have, on the road to their individuation, had to accept one of the collective functions, will not find it difficult to adapt themselves to society by a harmless attitude, as the collective function engenders the adaptation to life. So there must exist in the Club one trend which seeks a simple sociability by way of a so-called harmless unprejudiced attitude.

Among those however who are engaged in Analysis, where will be those who will be forced to go their own ways and who, through the acceptance of these ways, will feel themselves very much alone in the outer world. Just these will feel the wish to be taken up in the Club in the hope of finding there others who share their lot, thus finding an understanding which will make their path easier. These will also feel the need of sociability but the finding of a society wherein they will feel themselves at home, will depend on certain conditions. Giving up these conditions can be compared with a regression, – and this sociability is not to be reached through a harmless attitude, – its acceptance would be the same as doing violence to the newly acquired point of view.

Still a third difficulty must be mentioned here. In the Club both Analysts and patients can meet, but a really harmless intercourse between patients and Analysts is only possible when the patient has fully developed his individuation and can therefore hold his own toward his analyst. In the work with the Analyst and through him the patient learns to know himself. The resistances which develop during the work have their value, – they serve as indications and also in the breaking of the transference. They must therefore not be over-looked. For this reason too, many patients will not feel at ease in the society of the analysts and their wish to avoid them must be respected for their own good.

A forced 'harmlessness' only leads to an excessive extraversion which fortunately, in turn leads to the insight that the real path does not and cannot lie here, – but what is still more dangerous for the development of the individual, is that a forced harmlessness often leads to a, one might say, kind of incestuous collectivity, – a kind of 'Euphorie', in which the person overrates himself, and imagines he has reached a phase of development which has only been stolen by way of an unconscious identification.

For this reason I cannot agree with Dr. Jung when he says that the real Club will be formed by those seeking a simple sociability through a harmless attitude. In the Club there should be room for every kind of sociability, – and the way in which this society expresses itself should be determined by the original groups (Kerngruppen).

The Pension in which the Home exists as an original group, is annexed to the Club and has been created for those who wish to live in the Club. The principles which pertain to the Club should pertain also to the Pension and to the Home. The Home is in reality a differentiation of the Pension, and is therefore to be considered as an original group. The freedom to build these original groups should be accepted as one of the Club principles.

Beside the trend (Strömung) which looks for a simple sociability, there is another working hard at the reorganization of the Club and at introducing certain principles for its organization. To these principles, which seem to me to be condensed in Frl. Teucher's work, we must give serious consideration. These principles have grown out of the experiences gained in the life of the Club, and largely coincide with those principles which have developed logically out of the Libido theory of the Zurich School. Therefore just here an understanding should be possible, – theory and practice could be united.

It seems to me that the life of the Club will be expressed most largely by those who are in the midst of their Analysis, and who will find their way back to their old collectivity through the life at the Club. For those who have found their adaptation to life, the Club will be a too narrow collectivity.

I must say that outside the Club I find great values that the Club itself could never offer me, – and yet it would seem to me a pity if the Club did not exist.

Perhaps it might be well to give all members an opportunity to meet once or twice in the year at a simple meal at the Club, – less for the sake of the simple meal than to give the members a chance to meet and to create a milieu out of which the original groups could be formed. I should like to adopt Mr. McCormick's fantasy and to express the wish that the Club may develop in the direction of the Zurich School, and that the principles of the Libido-theory may also be introduced in the Club.

The collective-principle should tolerate the Individual-principle as its equal, and the goal of the Club should be the creating of a real analytical collectivity.

Zurich, 1917.[8]

---

8 English copy in the papers of the Analytical Psychology Club, New York.

Appendix III:

OF SCHOLARSHIP

A partial and journalistic account of the inception of my researches on 'Analytical collectivity' first appeared in John Kerr's review of *The Jung Cult* in the *London Review of Books*. As this generated several subsequent letters, a brief comment is in order. On first reading 'Analytical collectivity' in 1990, I formed a provisional hypothesis that it was actually Jung's inaugural address to the Psychological Club in Zürich. At that time I knew nothing concerning the history of the Club, and little about Jung's early circle. Since then, I have explored many hypothesis concerning the identity of the author and the significance of the text, as detailed in this book. I confided my initial hypothesis to John Kerr. Some time later, unbeknown to me, he passed this information on to Richard Noll. According to Kerr, though Noll had read 'Analytical collectivity', he had not realised its potential significance.[1] Noll subsequently incorporated it in the manuscript of *The Jung Cult*. When Kerr learnt of this, he claims that Noll agreed to remove the text at his request. He alleges that Noll broke a promise he made to him, and did not carry this out.[2] In a letter to the *London Review of Books*, Noll disputes Kerr's allegations. He asserts that prior to talking to Kerr, he had already identified the text as being by Jung and that it was a lecture to the Club. Kerr had merely confirmed what he already knew.[3] I reproduce here my letter in reply to Kerr's review:

> There is a time honoured institution by which publishers send manuscripts for peer review to anonymous reviewers.

---

1 John Kerr, 'Madnesses', p. 6.
2 Cited in Scott Heller, 'Flare-up over Jung', p. A16.
3 Noll, letter to the editor *London Review of Books*, 20 April 1995, p. 4.

The implications are serious when such procedures are contravened and compounded when such readers subsequently come to publish public reviews of these works and neglect to mention the full nature of their prior involvement.

In his review of Richard Noll's *The Jung Cult: Origins of a Charismatic Movement* (Princeton University Press, 1994), (*LRB* March 23rd) John Kerr gives an account of how a document that I provisionally identified as being by Jung came to appear in the aforementioned book. According to him it features as Noll's prime documentary evidence that under the guise of founding a school of psychology, Jung in actuality founded a cult akin to those around Luc Jouret and David Koresh, as Noll claimed in his piece in the *New York Times* (15th October, 1994).

Contrary to the impression given by Kerr's account, my research has led me to conclude that the thesis that the document constitutes the inauguration of a 'Jung cult' is quite erroneous. Noll's transcription of the document in his book is appallingly corrupt: handwritten additions in various hands are not distinguished from the typescript, and all are attributed to the sole authorship of Jung. Further, Noll's account is riddled with errors. To cite but one, he states that the document was evidently mailed by Maria Moltzer to Fanny Bowditch Katz in America (p. 250). Why would Moltzer have done this, when at the time in question Katz's address was Bergheimstrasse 8, Zürich? Contrary to Kerr's evaluation, the injured party is not myself, but responsible scholarship, which has once more taken a back seat to journalistic sensationalism.

In my view, an understanding of the document in question requires a contextualisation of Jung's work within the myriad attempts to establish dynamic psychologies of the unconscious from the last quarter of the nineteenth century onwards, coupled with detailed research in European archives. This is lacking in Noll's work, but has been accomplished in an outstanding manner by Fernando Vidal in his biography of Jung's Swiss compatriot *Piaget Before Piaget* (Harvard University Press, 1994).

Kerr states that after he read Noll's manuscript, in which Noll had utilised the document, he understood that Noll would remove all references to it. He neglects to mention that he read the manuscript in the capacity of an official

outside reader for Princeton University Press. His conversations with Noll took place at this time.

When I was informed that the document was to appear in
the book, I requested Noll to send me the relevant sections
of his manuscripts to judge for myself whether Kerr's
account of the appropriation of information (of which I had
just learnt) was true. He refused to do so. When Kerr learnt
that Noll had no intention of removing the document from
his book, he officially reversed his reader's report. This
forms the hidden history of his review.[4]

When I finally got to read *The Jung Cult*, it was clear to me that
Noll's understanding of 'analytical collectivity' bore no relation to
my own, and I consequently took no further action, and simply
continued my research.[5]

Inaccuracies in Noll's transcription of the document were also
independently pointed out by Paul Bishop in a letter to the *London
Review of Books*:

> It should be noted that there are at least 12 inconsistencies
> between the original document and the version published in
> Noll's book, some of which have been pointed out by the
> Jung scholar William McGuire. Most of these, as well as the
> changes in punctuation, are minor, but two – the replace-
> ment of 'devined' by 'defined', and the omission of the

---

4 Letter to the editor, *London Review of Books*, 20 April 1995, p. 4. Vidal's book and
   Eugene Taylor's *William James on Consciousness beyond the Margin* form the best
   recent works in the history of psychology. For an appreciation, see my
   'Psychology before psychology? A Review of *Piaget before Piaget* by Fernando
   Vidal'.

5 In January 1997, Noll hosted a week long cyberseminar on the Jung-Psyc mailing
   list run by John Hollwitz. Andrew Samuels sent in a reply which attempted to
   rebut Noll's accusations that he dishonestly critiqued the concept of the collective
   unconscious in private but not in public. Samuels tried to provide references to his
   published critiques of the concept. His reply included a question about how Noll
   reacted to the charges in the *London Review of Books* referred to above. As
   Samuels recounts, his contribution was rejected by Hollwitz, the moderator of the
   Jung-psyc list, who stated that such questions were *ad hominem* attacks. Although
   he did not agree with this evaluation, he removed the offending portions and was
   informed his piece had been accepted. But mysteriously it never appeared.
   Andrew Samuels, 'A bad experience on the internet'.

sentence 'The recognition and the acceptance of the personal life's task leads to the *Menschwerdung*' – might be considered more important.[6]

Later the same year, my letter was cited by John Peck in an article in the Swiss magazine *Du* on Jung's reception in the USA. Peck's article drew a rejoinder from Noll, who accused him of making legally slanderous remarks about his ethics. Noll stated that I made 'wild claims' about the inaccuracies in his book.[7] I leave readers to judge this for themselves, on the basis of the substance of this book. Concerning the transcription of the text, Noll wrote that errors of punctuation and a sentence which was omitted from the 'rushed first edition' were corrected, but that these did not affect the meaning of the document in anyway.[8] He added that he was 'unjustly accused by me' of appropriating my intellectual property and that I claimed that I was being victimised.[9] As is clear to anyone who reads my letter printed above, this was the diametric opposite of what I wrote, and a complete misrepresentation. Also, my request to Noll was simply to see a copy of the manuscript to ascertain for myself whether John Kerr's allegations, subsequently detailed in his emendation of his reader's report, were true. Peck replied as follows to Noll's letter:

Dr. Noll claims that he has not mishandled Jung's texts. He suggests that I have slandered him, and he invites me, in the interest of truth, to render apology. He does admit that changes in his printing of Jung's 1916 speech from a transcript originally in English, are now entering a second edition of his *The Jung Cult*. In his letter to 'du' he claims that these changes do not alter the meaning of the document 'one iota'. I have contacted the editors of Princeton University Press, who confirm that the form of one sentence in particular has been restored. This particular change was made at the request of the Jung family and 'with the permission of Richard Noll'. The sentence as Dr. Noll originally printed it, on p. 253 of his book, reads: 'there must be an

6 Paul Bishop, Letter to the editor, *London Review of Books,* 20 April 1995, p. 4
7 Noll, Letter to editor, *Du,* November 1995, p. 3
8 *Ibid.*
9 *Ibid.*

analytical Club that has perfect freedom to build an endless number of small groups'. As they stand, these words out of their context could suggest that a cult was in the making.

Dr. Noll introduced the transcript of Jung's 1916 speech by saying that with this speech 'the Jung cult of redemption and rebirth was formalized' (p. 250), and that through it one can see a 'program for spiritual revitalization' and even the sentiment for a possible postwar 'opening for the Jungians to step in and grab the world's attention'. Jung's reported sentence on group formation, as first printed by Dr. Noll, would seem to suit such a program. And Dr. Noll's introductory remarks make it clear that this document holds a signal place in the case that he wishes to build. The context for the sentence, however, simply describes the need of individual persons in the Club to form their own affiliations within its circle. In its restored form, the sentence now reads: 'there must be in an analytical Club that perfect freedom to build an endless number of small groups'. . . . Dr. Noll would also persuade us that the iotas of his textual changes in the 1916 transcript of Jung's speech make no difference. I leave readers of both his book and the record to form their own opinions.[10]

For a number of years, I have been researching a work on Jung and the making of modern psychology. During this period, I have located numerous interesting and unknown texts, which I intend to publish in the course of time. In his letter to *Du*, Noll alleged that I was 'merely sore' not to be the first to publish the text.[11] This is not true. In the course of my research I have endeavoured to conduct responsible scholarship, and not to publish until I have exhausted all possible avenues of inquiry. I had no interest in publishing 'Analytical collectivity' until – at the very least – I had conclusive evidence who it was by. It is for this reason that although I came across the text in 1990, it was not until 1997 that I felt that I had sufficiently researched all the avenues available to me and was prepared to publish my conclusions, which are presented in this book.

Since Peck's letter, new editions of Noll's book have appeared, in

10 John Peck, Letter to the editor, *Du* 3, 1996, p. 2.
11 Noll, Letter to the editor, *Du*, November 1995, p. 3.

which he has indeed altered the transcription of 'Analytical collectivity'. In the paperback edition of his book, Noll notes that minor errors in the transcription had been corrected.[12] If minor inaccuracies have been corrected, major ones remain. There are still alterations in punctuation – over twenty commas and dashes alone are omitted. Crossed out and handwritten words are not indicated. Whilst some of these points may not substantially alter the content of the text for purposes of interpretation, they are nevertheless of importance for purposes of identification – particularly so in deciding whether one is to regard it as an original manuscript, an original translation, or a copy. In particular, the frequent use of a comma followed by a dash is omitted. Significantly, this usage is also frequently found in Bowditch Katz's diaries and in Moltzer's 'The relation between the Zürich School and the Club'.

In *The Aryan Christ*, Noll has finally stated that the text contains 'corrections in an unknown hand' which have been included in his citations.[13] In this instance, I do not think this is sufficiently scholarly. Consequently, I have appended my own transcription of the document.

I also reproduce here a letter jointly written by Alan Elms and myself which corrects a further misstatement of Noll:

> In the paperback edition of *The Jung Cult*, Richard Noll states that 'credit for the original research [on *Memories, Dreams, Reflections*] must go to Alan Elms'.[14] Elms' research was published in 1994, and not 1974 as Noll erroneously states. We conducted our researches independently at the same time. When we learnt of each other's researches, we exchanged pre-publication drafts of our papers, as the cross-references indicate. Consequently, there is no issue of priority.[15]
>
> Alan Elms and Sonu Shamdasani

The problem with erroneous claims is the amount of time required to correct them – time which could otherwise be put to establishing a

---

12 Noll, *The Jung Cult*, p. xi, Fontana edition.
13 Noll, *The Aryan Christ*, p. 311.
14 Noll, *The Jung Cult*, Fontana edition, p. 301.
15 Alan Elms, 'The auntification of Jung', in *Uncovering Lives: The Uneasy Alliance of Biography and Psychology*; Sonu Shamdasani, 'Memories, dreams, omissions'.

proper account which has not had to start from questions which have been inadequately posed in the first place. In my view, there is much else that is erroneous in *The Jung Cult* and *The Aryan Christ*. I believe this book suffices to indicate their general unreliability, and that I have done enough to set the record straight so as not to have to be detained by them any longer. As Jung asked in 1944, 'Why don't people read my books conscientiously? Why do they gloss over the facts?'[16] Why indeed?

16 Jung to Herr Irminger, 22 September 1944, *Letters 1*, p. 347.

BIBLIOGRAPHY

Adler, Alfred. *Über den Nervösen Charakter: Grundzüge einer vergleichenden Individualpsychologie und Psychotherapie*, kommentierte textritische Ausgabe, ed. K.-H. Witte, A. Bruder-Bezzel, R. Kühn, Göttingen, Vanendhoeck & Ruprecht, 1997.

Ammann, Emile. 'Driving Miss Edith', tr. A. K. Donaghue, *Spring* 52, 1992, pp. 1–19.

Astor, James. *Michael Fordham: Innovations in Analytical Psychology*, London, Routledge, 1995.

Barker, Sarah. 'The Club problem', unpublished, 1918.

Baumann, Dieter, 'In memory of Franz Riklin', *Spring* 1970, pp. 1–6.

Bishop, Paul. *The Dionysian Self: C. G. Jung's Reception of Nietzsche*, Berlin, Walter de Gruyter, 1995.

—— Letter to the editor, *London Review of Books*, 20 April 1995, p. 4.

Burnham, John C. *Jeliffe: American Psychoanalyst and Physician & His Correspondence with Sigmund Freud and C. G. Jung* ed. W. McGuire, Chicago, University of Chicago Press, 1983.

Casement, Ann. 'A brief history of Jungian splits in the United Kingdom', *Journal of Analytical Psychology* 40, 1995, pp. 327–42.

Charet, F.X. *Spiritualism and the Foundations of C. G. Jung's Psychology*, Albany, State University of New York, 1993.

Collier, Peter and David Horowitz. *The Rockefellers: An American Dynasty*, London, Jonathan Cape, 1976.

Coward, Harold. *Jung and Eastern Thought*, with contributions by J. Borelli, J. Jordens and J. Henderson, New York, State University of New York Press, 1985.

Cunningham, Adrian. 'Victor White, John Layard and C. G. Jung', *Harvest: Journal for Jungian Studies* 38, 1992, pp. 44–57.

—— Review of Richard Noll, *The Jung Cult, Harvest: Journal for Jungian Studies* 41, 1995, pp. 99–104.

Donat, James G. 'Is depth psychology really deep? Reflections on the history of Jungian psychology'. *Harvest: Journal for Jungian Studies* 40, 1994, pp. 193–208.

Eliade, Mircea (ed) *The Encyclopedia of Religion*, vol. 4., New York, Macmillan, 1987.

Ellenberger, Henri. 'La Psychiatrie Suisse III', *Evolution psychiatrique*, 1952, pp. 139–58; 'La Psychiatrie Suisse VI' 1953, pp. 299–318.

—— *The Discovery of the Unconscious: The History and Evolution of Dynamic Psychiatry*, New York, Basic Books, 1997.

Elms, Alan. *Uncovering Lives: The Uneasy Alliance of Biography and Psychology*, New York, Oxford University Press, 1994.

Falzeder, Ernst. 'The threads of psychoanalytic filiations or psychoanalysis taking effect', in A. Haynal and E. Falzeder (eds), *100 Years of Psychoanalysis: Contributions to the History of Psychoanalysis*, special issue of *Cahiers Psychiatriques Genevois* 1994.

Flournoy, Théodore. *From India to the Planet Mars: A Case of Multiple Personality with Imaginary Languages*, ed. S. Shamdasani, with foreword by C. G. Jung and commentary by Mireille Cifali, tr. D. Vermilye, Princeton, Princeton University Press, 1899/1994.

Fordham, Michael. Letter to the editor, *British Medical Journal*, 29 August 1942, p. 260.

—— *The Objective Psyche*, London, Routledge & Kegan Paul, 1958.

—— *Explorations into the Self*, London, Academic Press, 1985.

—— *The Making of an Analyst*, London, Free Associations, 1993.

—— *Analyst–Patient Interaction: Collected Papers on Technique*, ed. S. Shamdasani, London, Routledge, 1996.

Fowler, H. W. *A Dictionary of Modern English Usage*, Oxford, Oxford University Press, 1926.

Foster, John. *Enquiry into the Practice and Effects of Scientology*, House of Commons Report 52, London, HMSO, December 1971.

Freud, Sigmund. *The Standard Edition of the Complete Psychological Works of Sigmund Freud*, ed. & tr. J. Strachey London, Hogarth Press, 1953–74.

Freud, Sigmund and Binswanger, Ludwig. *Sigmund Freud Ludwig Binswanger Briefwechsel 1908–1939*, ed. G. Fichtner, Frankfurt am Main, S. Fischer, 1992.

Freud, Sigmund and Ferenczi, Sándor. *The Correspondence of Sigmund Freud and Sándor Ferenczi, Volume 1, 1908–1914*, ed. E. Brabant, E. Falzeder & P. Giampieri-Deutsch, tr. P. Hoffer, Cambridge, Harvard University Press, 1993.

—— *The Correspondence of Sigmund Freud and Sándor Ferenczi, Volume 2, 1914–1919*, ed. E. Falzeder and E. Brabant, tr. P. Hoffer, Cambridge, Harvard University Press, 1996.

Freud, Sigmund and Jung, C. G. *The Freud/Jung Letters*, ed. W. McGuire, tr. R. Mannheim and R. F. C. Hull. Princeton, Princeton University Press and London, Hogarth Press/Routlege & Kegan Paul, 1974.

Galanter, Marc. *Cults: Faith, Healing and Coercion*, New York, Oxford University Press, 1989.

Grimaldi-Craig, Sheila. 'I want my money back', review of Richard Noll, *The Jung Cult*, *Spring: A Journal of Archetype and Culture*, pp. 143–50.

Goethe, Johann Wolfgang von. *Goethes Werk* vol. 2, ed. E. Trunz, Hamburg, Christian Wegner Verlag, 1952.

—— *Faust I & II, Collected Works*, vol. 2, tr. S. Atkins, Princeton, Princeton University Press, 1994.

Hannah, Barbara. *C. G. Jung: His Life and Work. A Biographical Memoir*, New York, Perigree, 1976.

Haule, John. 'From somnambulism to the archetypes: the French roots of Jung's split from Freud', *Psychoanalytic Review* 1984, pp. 635–59.

Heller, Scott. 'Flare-up over Jung: dispute involves an author, a university press, and a psychoanalyst's heirs', *Chronicle of Higher Education*, June 16 1995, pp. A9 and A16.

Heisig, James. *Imago Dei: A Study of Jung's Psychology of Religion*, Lewisburg, Bucknell University Press, 1979.

Hersch, Michael, 'Worldwide, it's the "rush hour of the Gods": a clamor for cultic meaning in a society gone secular', *Newsweek*, April 14 1997, p. 19.

Hexham, Irving and Poewe, Karla. *New Religions and Global Cultures: Making the Human Sacred*, Boulder, Westview Press, 1997.

Jacobi, Jolande. *The Psychology of C. G. Jung: An Introduction with Illustrations*, tr. R. Manheim, London, Routledge & Kegan Paul, 1968.

Jung, C. G. *Die Psychologie der unbewussten Prozesse: Ein Überblick über die moderne Theorie und Methode der analytichsen Psychologie*, Zurich, Rascher, 1918, 2nd edn; 'The psychology of the unconscious processes', in ed. C. Long, *Collected Papers on Analytical Psychology*, London, Baillière, Tindall & Cox, 1917, 2nd edn., pp. 354–444.

—— *Collected Works*, ed. Sir H. Read, M. Fordham, G. Adler and W. McGuire, tr. R. Hull, Bollingen Series, Princeton, Princeton University Press and London, Routledge, 1944-.

—— *Modern Psychology 3 & 4. The Process of Individuation: 3 Eastern Texts / 4 Exercetia spiritualia of St. Ignatius of Loyola. Notes on Lectures given at the Eidgenössische Technische Hochschule, Zürich by Prof. Dr. C. G. Jung, October 1938 – March 1940*, Zurich, 1959, 2nd edn.

—— *C. G. Jung Letters*, selected and ed. G. Adler in collaboration with A. Jaffé, tr. R. F. C. Hull, Bollingen Series XCV, Princeton, Princeton University Press and London, Routledge, 1973, 1975, 2 vols.

—— *Memories, Dreams, Reflections*, 1963, London, Flamingo, 1983.

—— *Analytical Psychology: Notes of the Seminar given in 1925*, ed. W. McGuire, Bollingen Series XCIX, Princeton, Princeton University Press and London, Routledge, 1989.

—— *The Psychology of Kundalini Yoga: Notes of the Seminar given in 1932 by C. G. Jung*, ed. S. Shamdasani, Bollingen Series XCIX, Princeton, Princeton University Press and London, Routledge, 1996.

Kempis, Thomas À. *The Imitation of Christ*, tr. B. Knott, London, Fount, 1996.

Kerr, John. 'Madnesses', review of Richard Noll, *The Jung Cult*, *The London Review of Books*, 23 March 1995, pp. 3–6.

Kirsch, Thomas, review of Richard Noll, *The Jung Cult*, *Psychoanalytic Review*, 82, 1995, pp. 793–7.

La Rosa, Leo. Letter to the editor, *Journal of Analytical Psychology* 41, 1996, pp. 289–90.

Lammers, Ann Conrad. *In God's Shadow: The Collaboration between Victor White and C. G. Jung*, New York, Paulist Press, 1994.

Ljunggren, Magnus. *The Russian Mephisto: A Study of the Life of Emilii Medtner*, Stockholm, Almqvist & Wiksell International, 1994.

McGuire, William and Hull, R. F. C. *C. G. Jung Speaking: Interviews and Encounters*, Bollingen Series XCVII, Princeton, Princeton University Press, 1977.

Medtner, Emil. 'Bildnis der Persönlichkeit im Rahmen des gegenseitigen sich Kennenlernens', in *Die Kulturelle Bedeutung der Komplexen Psychologie*, ed. Psychological Club Zurich, Berlin, Julius Springer, 1935, pp. 516–616.

Meier, C. A. *Ancient Incubation and Modern Psychotherapy*, tr. M. Curtis, Evanston, Northwestern University Press, 1967.

Muser, Friedel. *Zur Geschichte der Psychologischen Clubs Zürich von den Anfangen bis 1928*, Zurich, Psychological Club, 1984.

Nagy, Marilyn. *Philosophical Issues in the Psychology of C. G. Jung*, Albany, State University of New York Press, 1991.

—— 'The truth of the matter', review of Richard Noll, *The Jung Cult*, *San Francisco Jung Institute Library Journal*, 14, 1995, pp. 25–28.

Noll, Richard. 'The rose, the cross and the analyst', op. ed. column, *New York Times*, 15 October 1994.

—— Letter to the editor, *London Review of Books*, 20 April 1995, p. 4.

—— Letter to the editor, *Du*, November 1995, p. 3.

—— *The Jung Cult: The Origins of a Charismatic Movement*, Princeton, Princeton University Press, 1994; London, Fontana, 1996.

—— *The Aryan Christ: The Secret Life of Carl Jung*, New York, Random House, 1997.

Peck, John. 'Die Rezeption in den USA', *Du* 8, 1995, pp. 88–96.

—— Letter to the editor. *Du* March 1996, p. 2.

Psychological Club, Zurich. *Jahresbericht* 1917.

Samuels, Andrew. ' "A Jung Club is not enough": the professionalisation of Analytical Psychology 1913–1957 and its implications for today', *Harvest: Journal for Jungian Studies*, 40, 1994, pp.155–67.

—— 'A bad experience on the internet', 1997, http://www.cgjung.com/techsam1.html.

Shamdasani, Sonu. 'Two unknown early cases of Jung'. *Harvest: Journal for Jungian Studies*, 38, 1992, pp. 38–43.

—— 'Memories, Dreams, Omissions', *Spring: Journal of Archetype and Culture* 57, 1995, pp. 115–137.

—— Letter to the editor, *London Review of Books*, 20th April, 1995, p. 4.

—— 'Psychology before psychology?' review of *Piaget before Piaget* by Fernando Vidal, *San Fransisco Jung Institute Library Journal*, 15, 3, 1996, pp. 21–26.

—— 'De Genève à Zürich: Jung et la Suisse Romande', *Revue médicale de la Suisse Romande*, vol. 116, 1996, pp. 917–22; 'From Geneva to Zürich: Jung and French Switzerland', *Journal of Analytical Psychology*, forthcoming.

—— 'La folie du jour: Jung et ses cas', in *Histoire de la psychiatrie: Nouvelles approches, nouvelles perspectives*, ed. V. Barras and J. Gasser, Paris, Les empêcheurs de penser en rond, forthcoming.

—— 'Psychoanalysis Inc'. in *Medicine in the Twentieth Century*, ed. J. Pickstone and R. Cooter, Harwood, forthcoming.

Sherry, Jay. 'Case not proven', review of Richard Noll, *The Jung Cult*, *San Francisco Jung Institute Library Journal* 14, 1995, pp. 17–23.

Skues, Richard. 'The first casualty: the war over psychoanalysis and the poverty of historiography', *History of Psychiatry*, forthcoming.

Smith, Dinita. 'Scholar who says Jung lied is at war with descendants', *New York Times*, 3 June 1995, pp. 1 and 9.

Stern, Paul J. *C. G. Jung: The Haunted Prophet*, New York, George Braziller, 1976.

Storr, Anthony. *Feet of Clay: A Study of Gurus*, London, HarperCollins, 1996.

Taylor, Eugene. 'C. G. Jung and the Boston psychopathologists, 1902–1912', in *Carl Jung and Soul Psychology*, ed. E. M. Stern, New York, Haworth Press, 1986, pp. 131–44.

Thornton, Edward. *The Diary of a Mystic*, London, George Allen & Unwin, 1967.

Vidal, Fernando. *Piaget before Piaget*, Cambridge, Harvard University Press, 1994.

Webb, James. *The Occult Establishment vol II: The Age of Irrational*, London, Richard Drew, 1976/1981.

Wittenberger, Gerhard. *Das 'Geheime Komitee' Sigmund Freuds: Institutionalisierungsprozesse in der Psychoanalytischen Bewegung zwischen 1912 und 1927'*, Tübingen, Editions Diskord, 1995.

Wulff, Martin. *Psychology of Religion: Classic and Contemporary Views*, New York, John Wiley, 1990.

INDEX